PENGUIN BOOKS

THE FIRST EMPEROR OF CHINA

Arthur Cotterell was born in Berkshire in 1942. He was educated at Ashmead School, Reading, and St John's College, Cambridge. Now Principal of Kingston College of Further Education in Surrey, he combines a career in education and training after school with an extensive interest in other civilizations, many of them ancient. His published works include *The Minoan World*, *A Dictionary of World Mythology*, *The Encyclopedia of Ancient Civilizations* and *China: A Concise, Cultural History*. At present he is writing a general history of East Asia, an area in which he is well travelled.

Arthur Cotterell is married with one son and lives in Surrey.

秦始皇帝

THE
FIRST EMPEROR
OF CHINA

ARTHUR COTTERELL

Introduction by
Mr Yang Chen Ching
Curator of the Museum of Warrior and Horse Figures
from the tomb of Ch'in Shih-huang-ti

PENGUIN BOOKS

PENGUIN BOOKS

Published by the Penguin Group
27 Wrights Lane, London W8 5TZ, England
Viking Penguin Inc., 40 West 23rd Street, New York, New York 10010, USA
Penguin Books Australia Ltd, Ringwood, Victoria, Australia
Penguin Books Canada Ltd, 2801 John Street, Markham, Ontario, Canada L3R 1B4
Penguin Books (NZ) Ltd, 182–190 Wairau Road, Auckland 10, New Zealand

Penguin Books Ltd, Registered Offices: Harmondsworth, Middlesex, England

First published in Great Britain by Macmillan London Ltd 1981
Published in the USA in Penguin Books 1988
Published in Great Britain in Penguin Books 1989

Made and printed in Singapore by
Toppan Printing Co. (S) PTE. Ltd

CONTENTS

Preface   7

Introduction *by Mr Yang Chen Ching*
Curator of the Museum of Warrior and Horse Figures
from the tomb of Ch'in Shih-huang-ti   9

PART ONE   The Archaeological Discoveries

Chapter One   The Tomb of Ch'in Shih-huang-ti   16

Chapter Two   The Land within the Passes; Hsienyang and the Wei river valley   54

PART TWO   The Historical Context

Chapter Three   Feudal Decline; the Ch'un Ch'iu period, 770–481 BC   84

Chapter Four   The Triumph of Ch'in; the Chan Kuo period, 481–221 BC   101

Chapter Five   An Age of Intellectual Turmoil   118

PART THREE   The Ch'in Empire

Chapter Six   Ch'in Shih-huang-ti, the First Emperor of China   136

Chapter Seven   Li Ssu, Grand Councillor and Guiding Genius of Ch'in   158

Chapter Eight   The Fall of the Ch'in Dynasty   177

Chronologies   195

Bibliography   198

List of Maps and Plans   202

Acknowledgments   203

Permissions   205

Index   206

To the enduring genius of the Chinese people

PREFACE

This volume is a study of China's unifier, Ch'in Shih-huang-ti, the First Emperor, who was the sole ruler from 221 to 210 BC. Although no Chinese sovereign arouses more controversy than the enigmatic First Emperor, Builder of the Great Wall and Burner of the Books, the impact of his short-lived dynasty on the history of ancient East Asia was profound and laid the foundation of a political system that lasted in China for two millennia. Fortunately for the biographer today, a wealth of new archaeological data has become available through the excavations at Mount Li, the site of the First Emperor's tomb. Since 1974 Chinese archaeologists have unearthed a life-size pottery army consisting of armoured infantry, crossbowmen, spearmen, charioteers and horsemen. These magnificent pieces of sculptured terracotta are now being patiently restored and exhibited where they were found. Over 7,000 figures are estimated to be in the four subterranean chambers that have been explored so far.

During the summer of 1980 I was able to visit the excavations at Mount Li, as a guest of the People's Republic of China. Along with my wife and son, I had the privilege of meeting the archaeologists and historians currently investigating the new finds. Every courtesy and assistance was offered by the Chinese authorities so that materials could be gathered for the present book, a generosity for which I shall remain forever indebted.

There are certain people, however, we must thank individually for their kindness and hospitality. First, Mr Jiang Nanxiang, Minister of Education, who took a personal interest in our visit, and Mr Qi Kuang, Vice-Director of the State Administrative Bureau of Museums and Archaeological Data, who lent his support to our research. In Peking we owe much also to the help of Mr Hu Shiu Hsin, Vice-Director of the Foreign Affairs Bureau of the Ministry of Education, Mr Kuo Lao Wei, Director of the Foreign Affairs Section of the State Administrative Bureau of Museums and Archaeological Data, and Mr Ma Dien Yuan, Responsible Member of the Liaison Section of the Bureau of Foreign Affairs of the Ministry of Education. In Sian our thanks are due to Mr Yang Da, Director of the Bureau of Museums and Archaeological Data of Shensi Province, and Mr Bieh Ding Eou, Director of the Foreign Affairs Section of the Provincial Bureau of Education. Two others must be specially mentioned. One is Mr Chen Hsin Po, from the Peking Foreign Languages Institute, our constant companion and helper; the other is Mr Yang Chen Ching, Curator of the Museum of Warrior and Horse Figures from the Tomb of Ch'in Shih-huang-ti, who spent much of his valuable time with us at Mount Li and subsequently even more in writing an introduction to this volume.

Closer to home I should like to acknowledge the invaluable assistance provided by my wife in translating from the Chinese.

Richmond upon Thames, January 1981

INTRODUCTION

Yang Chen Ching
Curator of the Museum of Warrior and Horse Figures from the tomb of Ch'in Shih-huang-ti

Long ago in 350 BC, when the people of feudal China suffered from the miseries of incessant warfare and yearned for peace and prosperity, King Hsiao of Ch'in took the advice of Shang Yang and reformed his state. Complying with the imperative of historical development, Ch'in kept its enemies at a distance and underwent a thorough internal reorganization, thereby beginning to transform itself from a backward state into one of the most powerful of the feudal kingdoms. In 246 BC Prince Cheng ascended the Ch'in throne and completed this process of reorganization by reforming the laws and strengthening the army. In the decade prior to 221 BC he succeeded in destroying all the other feudal states and unifying China. To celebrate the great event King Cheng adopted the title of Ch'in Shih-huang-ti, the First Emperor.

Ch'in Shih-huang-ti, the son of King Chuang-hsiang, was born in about 258 BC in Han-tan, the capital of the state of Chao. He lost his father when he was thirteen years old and he was obliged to suppress an armed uprising in 238 BC, the year he ceased having a regent. It was after this rebellion that he threw himself into a programme of reforms covering political, economic, cultural and military affairs. As a result the foundations were laid for the initial unification of the country.

The lessons of history are worth noting. Ch'in rose to dominance through human effort. Once the correct route was discovered, and all positive factors were mobilized and supported by workable measures, the state grew from strength to strength. In particular, the First Emperor made use of talent, gathering around him the able and only promoting the meritorious. His chief adviser was Li Ssu, not a native of Ch'in. Even Cheng Kuo first came as a spy to

Hsienyang, the Ch'in capital, though he subsequently contributed greatly to the state by overseeing the digging of a major drainage and irrigation scheme. The First Emperor also attended to matters personally. He was well informed about affairs of state, each day reading piles of reports and documents and he would not rest until he had finished with them. From 221 BC he controlled the empire through specially appointed officials who administered its thirty-six commanderies.

Not only did the First Emperor centralize government, but he also standardized ancient China's laws, currency, roads, weights and measures, axle lengths, and written language. This was necessary because each of the Seven States existing before unification had a different system. The First Emperor, however, was anxious to ensure that proper standards were maintained throughout his realm. The histories tell us that 'goods had to carry the maker's name, so as to ensure quality, for those who made faulty things were liable to punishment'. We find in the pits of the terracotta army at Mount Li that the bricks used for the floors have these marks on them.

For his army the First Emperor relied on the peasant farmers, who were given training in time of peace and rewards for bravery in time of war. According to the histories, 'the infantry and cavalry of Ch'in were great in number. The foot soldiers wore no helmets and engaged the enemy with untold ferocity. The mounts of the cavalry were so swift that they could jump twelve paces. Whereas the soldiers of the other feudal states when they entered the fray wore heavy armour which was clumsy and impeded their movements, the Ch'in soldiers threw away their coats of mail and charged headlong.' Government officials were generally military men, promoted for their war service. They remained intensely loyal to the First Emperor and governed the empire on his behalf.

The saying goes that to begin an enterprise is not easy but to keep hold of success is even more difficult. After unification the First Emperor believed that he was above comparison with anyone else; he was greater than the Five Emperors of old. This opinion led him to pursue still more ambitious aims. He sent armies to conquer the south of China, and to drive off the nomadic peoples threatening the northern frontier; he ordered the construction of a network of trunk roads and of the Great Wall; he drafted thousands of convicts

Mr Yang Chen Ching pointing to one of the exhibits at Mount Li museum.

to build the huge A-fang palace and his own mausoleum at Mount Li; and he used severe punishments to deal with any opposition, burning books and burying scholars alive in Hsienyang. On tours of inspection the First Emperor used to have long inscriptions set up extolling his achievements, so that future generations would praise his name. The concentration of the entire feudal nobility in specially built palaces at Hsienyang was doubtless intended to enhance his reputation too. All these great schemes of the First Emperor cost the country dearly. Probably 3,000,000 men were involved or 15 per cent of the population. The diversion of manpower caused a sharp drop in agricultural productivity, shaking the Ch'in empire to its foundations and preparing for the popular rebellions which overthrew it after the First Emperor's death. Assassination attempts not only failed to give the First Emperor reason to pause, but more they encouraged him to become aloof and curtail his public appearances. In fact, he dispatched emissaries to the immortals in order to obtain the elixir of life.

Even before the death of the First Emperor in 210 BC the empire was steeped in grievances. It was as though the land was covered with dry wood and awaited only a torch to start an uncontrollable blaze. The man who lit that fire was Chen She, a poor wage-labourer. It was not long before the Second Emperor and his successor, King Tzu-ying of Ch'in, were killed, and Hsienyang was burned to the ground. This first peasant insurrection in Chinese history revealed how a country depends on its people. The First Emperor's indifference to the welfare of his subjects had brought total destruction to his dynasty. It is a lesson to us all.

Today the excavations at Mount Li are also instructive. Our study of the terracotta figures and horses provides invaluable material for understanding Ch'in – its politics, economy, society, and military system. Looking at the remarkable finds, it is possible to recognize the high level of development then achieved in ancient China, thus encouraging the present generation to strive for the modernization of our country by the year 2000.

Because the Mount Li finds are of equal interest to the peoples of the world, I was pleased to meet Mr Cotterell on his visit to the site last year. He was collecting illustrative material for this book on the First Emperor, and we spent many hours talking about the

terracotta army and the unexcavated tomb mound. I am delighted
to write this introduction to his study now, and I hope that my
words assist readers in following the fascinating story of China's
unification.

——————

Mount Li, January 1981

PART ONE

THE
ARCHAEOLOGICAL
DISCOVERIES

Chapter One

The Tomb of Ch'in Shih-huang-ti

On our car journey to the tomb of the First Emperor at Mount Li, some forty kilometres (twenty-five miles) east of Sian, the capital of Shensi province, we passed through Lintong, the administrative centre of an area of intensive agriculture. Elderly men and children – the perennial grandfathers and grandchildren of China – spread maize to dry in the sun along the edge of the metalled highway, although on that hot July day the traffic was heavy with buses, lorries and horse-drawn waggons. After Lintong we turned off the main highway and drove between irrigated fields of corn and vegetables, until suddenly on the right appeared the tomb mound of the First Emperor, looking like a low hill. From the modern tree-lined road we could see the green tumulus and behind, the hazy outline of Mount Li itself. The grave is midway between the mountain and the

A close-up view of the steps leading to the tomb mound of Ch'in Shih-huang-ti. The author's son stands next to the sign indicating the size of the hill.

Wei river. The site would have been chosen in accordance with the ancient practices of geomancy, or what the Chinese call *feng-shui*, 'wind and water'. The occult knowledge of the Taoist geomancers was supposed to ensure that evil spirits did not trouble the deceased.

The tumulus has not yet been excavated. Its only known disturbance happened in 206 BC, when the rebellious peasant army of Hsiang Yu pillaged and burned everything it could find that was connected with the Ch'in dynasty. But we know from the writings of the Han historian, Ssu-ma Ch'ien (145—*c.* 90 BC), something of what the First Emperor intended his own mausoleum to be. In the *Shih Chi (Historical Records)* we read:

> As soon as the First Emperor became king of Ch'in [in 246 BC] work was begun on his mausoleum at Mount Li. After he won the empire [in 221 BC], more than 700,000 conscripts from all parts of China laboured there. They dug through three underground streams; they poured molten copper for the outer coffin; and they filled the burial chamber with models of palaces, towers and official buildings, as well as fine utensils, precious stones and rarities. Artisans were ordered to fix automatic crossbows so that grave robbers would be slain. The waterways of the empire, the Yellow and Yang-tzu rivers, and even the great ocean itself, were represented by mercury and were made to flow mechanically. Above, the heavenly constellations were depicted, while below lay a representation of the earth. Lamps using whale oil were installed to burn for a long time.
>
> The Second Emperor decreed [in 210 BC] that his father's childless concubines should follow him to the grave. After they were duly buried an official suggested that the artisans responsible for the mechanical devices knew too much about the contents of the tomb for safety. Therefore, once the First Emperor was placed in the burial chamber and the treasures were sealed up, the middle and outer gates were shut to imprison all those who had worked on the tomb. No one came out. Trees and grass were then planted over the mausoleum to make it look like a hill.

Leaving our Chinese hosts talking to my wife at the bottom of the mound, I struggled after my ten-year-old son up its steep side. The twisting path, little better than a series of footholds, climbs nearly fifty metres (164 feet) through fruit trees to the top. Once there,

17

Facing page:
This photograph is taken from the top of the tomb mound of Ch'in Shih-huang-ti. In the far distance is the hangar-like roof over Pit No. 1.

having got our breath back, we were struck by the size of the rammed earth hill, over 1,400 metres (4,593 feet) in circumference. Somewhere beneath our feet lay the mortal remains of Ch'in Shih-huang-ti, the unifier of China. It is doubtful whether he would have expected to have an orchard above his burial chamber as there is today, as the species then planted as grave trees were pines and cypresses. Both of these trees were also favoured for coffins, since the ancient Chinese prized the durability of their resinous wood as well as a certain vitality which they believed lingered in it. The latter quality was thought to be of invaluable assistance to the deceased. Perhaps the fact that neither scorching summer nor freezing winter ravages the foliage of the cypress and the pine led to the notion of a special store of energy. Alchemists were convinced that extracts of resin from particular trees would enable a person to live for five hundred years. Although the tumulus is today surrounded only by well-tended fields, in 210 BC there were two walled enclosures to protect the grave from the attention of marauders. Preliminary investigation has revealed that an inner wall pierced by four gates measures 685 by 578 metres (2,247 by 1,896 feet), and an outer wall 2,173 by 974 metres (7,129 by 3,196 feet); the total area enclosed must have been nearly two square kilometres (three-quarters of a square mile).

A number of funerary buildings were unearthed in March 1977 north of the modern road which bisects the mausoleum site, possibly a section of a 'sleeping' or 'death' palace. From records of later imperial burial customs we are aware that worshippers were settled on the site of an emperor's tomb in these specially constructed palaces. Apart from guards and servants raised from the neighbouring peasantry, a number of the emperor's concubines were usually drafted as warders of the grave and its garden. In the case of the First Emperor we cannot be sure of the identity of his funerary attendants, as the Second Emperor buried his childless concubines with him, but we may reasonably assume that Ch'in Shih-huang-ti did not radically depart from traditional practice. It would even seem that the First Emperor institutionalized grave sacrifice by erecting the first permanent funerary temple next to a tomb. The great mound now standing at Mount Li descends from the tumuli of earlier kings, its extraordinary bulk being merely an expression of the First Emperor's pride in the achievements of his unusual reign.

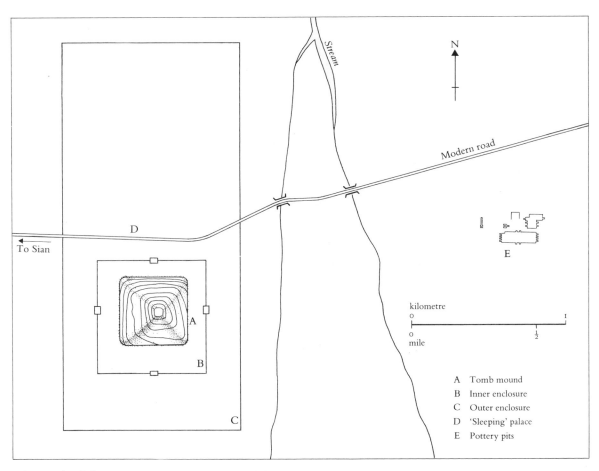

The tomb of the First Emperor at Mount Li

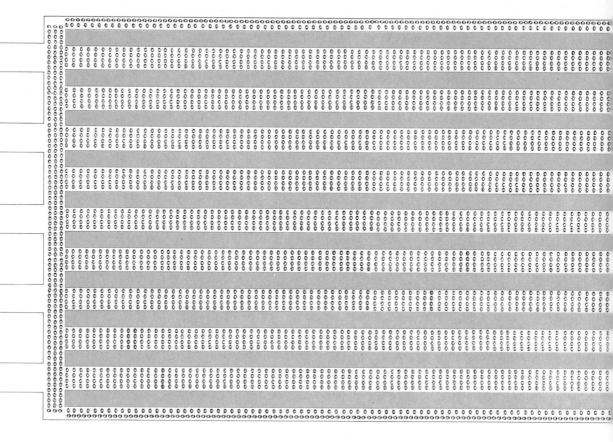

Looking eastwards from the top of this mound, we could see the hangar-like roof covering Pit No. 1 of the terracotta army one and a half kilometres (one mile) away. We scrambled down the footpath, paused for a backward glance at the foot of the slope, then rejoined our companions in the car. Within a few minutes we turned into the forecourt of the museum, to find Mr Yang Chen Ching, the curator, awaiting our arrival. On his head was the soft broad-rimmed hat worn by Shensi farmers, who know the power of the summer sun. After introductions and tea in his office, he kindly answered our questions about the amazing finds under his care.

As he explained, there are four pits altogether. Three of them contain pottery figures and horses; the other is empty. The largest one – known as Pit No. 1 – was discovered in March 1974, when a series of wells was excavated in search of water to supply the local community. The pit's shape is rectangular, and it measures about 210

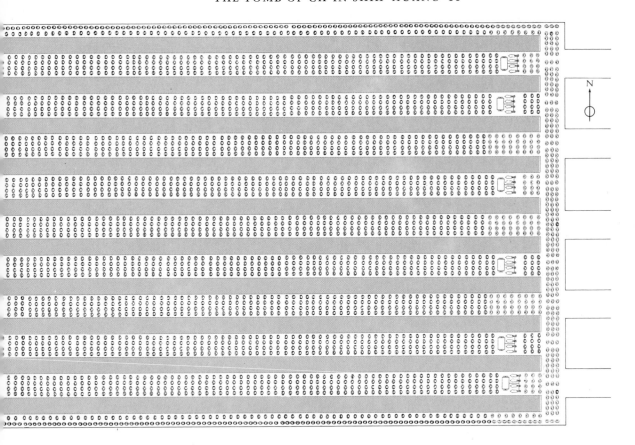

Plan of Pit No. 1.

⊙⊙⊙⊙ Unarmoured soldier

◖◗◖◗ Armoured soldier

Six chariots at east end

metres (689 feet) from east to west and 60 metres (197 feet) from north to south. It consists of a series of eleven parallel corridors, nine measuring 3 metres (10 feet) by 200 metres (656 feet), and two measuring just under 2 metres (7 feet) by 200 metres (656 feet). The narrower corridors run along the outside. At the east and west ends, a gallery runs from north to south, with five earthen ramps leading to the surface. There may have been two other entrances on the north and south sides as well. These subterranean chambers were skilfully built: the rammed earth surrounding the corridors and galleries prevented subsidence, while each chamber was paved with bricks and its wooden roof was supported by stout timber pillars and cross-beams. To prevent moisture seeping down from the surface, the roof was covered by woven matting and then a layer of clay. It is likely that the rebel soldiers were able to find the pits in 206 BC because the soil excavated from them rose in small tell-tale mounds.

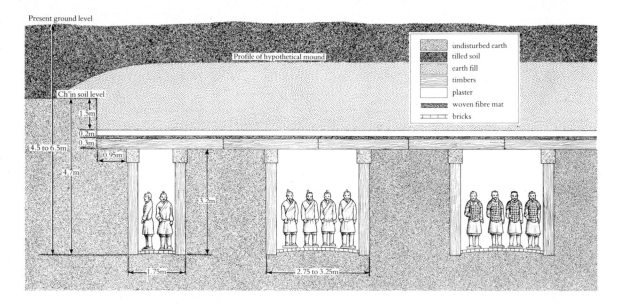

Present ground level

Profile of hypothetical mound

Ch'in soil level

undisturbed earth
tilled soil
earth fill
timbers
plaster
woven fibre mat
bricks

Cross-sectional views of
three corridors in Pit
No. 1.

No. 1 Pit is a military formation. The chambers are arranged in the battle order of an infantry regiment, which faces eastwards. Altogether it is estimated that there are 3,210 terracotta foot soldiers. They do not wear helmets; only Ch'in officers have these. But most of the infantry soldiers wear armour. These armoured men are divided into forty files; they stand four abreast in the nine wide corridors, and form two files in each of the narrow ones. The head of the regiment in the eastern gallery comprises a vanguard of unarmoured bowmen and crossbowmen, nearly 200 sharpshooters, drawn up in three north–south ranks. Their clothing is light cotton because they are fast moving, long-range fighters – the ancient equivalent of artillery. They would have fired their arrows from a distance, keeping away from hand-to-hand engagements, once contact was made with the enemy. The three ranks would have taken turns at firing, so as to keep up a continuous stream of arrows. The majority carried crossbows with a 200-metre (650-foot) shooting range.

Between these sharpshooters and the armoured infantry are six chariots and three unarmoured infantry squads. Each chariot is pulled by four terracotta horses and manned by a charioteer and one or two soldiers. The guards would have wielded long flexible lances, possibly bamboos measuring as much as six metres (twenty feet), in order to stop enemy soldiers from cutting off the heads of the horses.

Facing page:
A detailed photograph of
a corridor in Pit No. 1, at
the earliest stage of
excavation. The soldiers
are unarmoured
spearmen.

Facing page:
Pit No. 1.
The first ranks behind the vanguard of the infantry regiment are buried here.

Overleaf:
The tomb mound of the First Emperor with Mount Li in the background.

Below:
An unusually well-preserved example of chariot horses in Pit No. 1.

Two of the six chariots, however, seem to have had a special function. They were command vehicles, equipped with drums and bells. The officers riding on them could order the regiment to advance or retreat by striking these instruments. Officers wore headgear, mainly rode in chariots, and displayed badges of rank. Besides the groups of twelve unarmoured footmen who precede the six chariots, there are in the other three corridors squads containing thirty-two spearmen. Their spears might have been longer than the two-metre (seven-foot) ones belonging to the armoured infantry in the rear. Again these lightly dressed soldiers were probably mobile

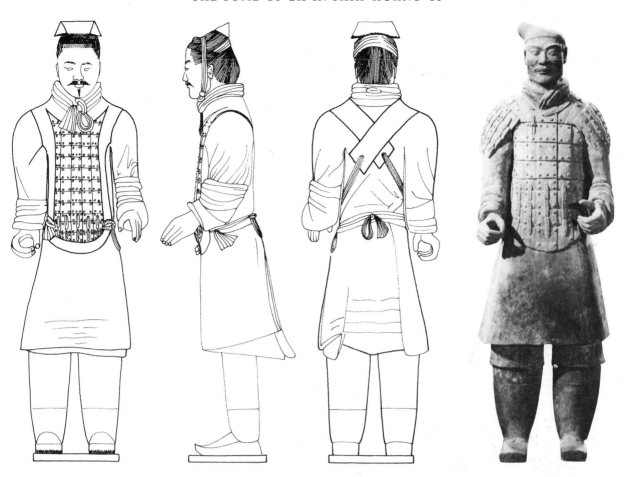

auxiliaries who co-operated with both the crossbowmen and the chariots.

In each of the narrow north and south corridors a line of soldiers faces outwards. Although these men were guarding the flanks, they have no shields. Ch'in soldiers did not use shields at all: their vigilance and bravery would have been thought sufficient protection on the battlefield. Even the armour worn by Ch'in troops covered only a relatively small portion of the body. This means that a regiment like the one in Pit No. 1 always took the offensive, always attacked. We know of the ferocity of Ch'in armies from the historical records, but not until these pottery figures were unearthed was it appreciated how much the strategy of Ch'in generals depended on taking the initiative on the battlefield. The troops under their command were certainly the most mobile of the time. They were also the best disciplined since

Above left:
Drawings of a charioteer from the second pit.

Above right:
A charioteer of a command vehicle in Pit No. 1. The toggle on the upper right-hand side indicates where the mail coat was fastened.

Facing page:
One of the officers from the command vehicles in the first pit. The Ch'in infantry was directed by such chariot-borne commanders.

the officers would not have hesitated to decapitate any soldier who disobeyed orders.

The terracotta soldiers definitely had real arms, Mr Yang Chen Ching believed, and they were probably made from bronze. Little iron has been recovered from the pits. All the pits, however, were plundered for weapons by the rebel forces after the downfall of the Ch'in dynasty. Despite all the looting and destruction, various bronze weapons such as arrow heads, halberds, spear heads, swords, and crossbow triggers have been found. Over 1,400 bronze arrow heads have been recovered in the trial excavation of Pit No. 2 alone. On the other hand, the armour of the terracotta soldiers, sculpted in detail on the pottery figures, suggests that iron may have been used for this purpose. Even the heads of the rivets on the coats of mail have been modelled. The histories tell us that during the Chan Kuo period both iron mail coats and iron weapons existed; furthermore, the remains of an actual coat of mail were excavated in 1965 in Hopei province. It consisted of numerous iron slates, joined so that the top pieces pressed on the ones below them. At Mount Li seven different styles of mail coat have been found. They are excellently designed and reveal the advanced nature of ancient Chinese protective weapons. The Chinese investigators have concluded that a mail coat was put on and taken off over the head, the button for fastening it

Facing page:
Bolts or crossbow arrow heads as they were unearthed.

A bronze crossbow trigger mechanism recovered from Pit No. 1.

27

Rear view of a Ch'in warrior. The characters stamped on the base of the skull may refer to the soldier's name or to that of the potter-sculptor.

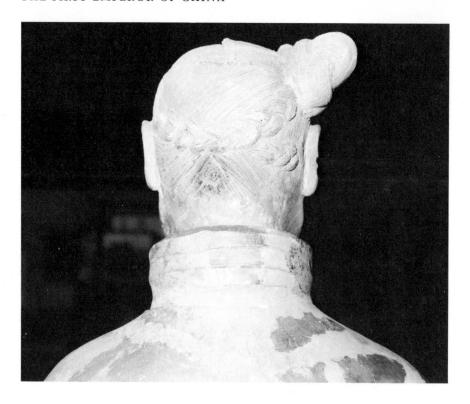

tight being on the upper right side, where the coat opens and closes.

The statues in Pit No. 1 are made from the heavy clay found in the vicinity of Mount Li. The advantage for the Ch'in potter-sculptor was that this type of clay was strong enough for large-scale pieces. Although some people find this difficult to believe, no two faces are alike. Each head is a personal portrait, and so far the excavators have not discovered two faces which are the same. Unlike the stereotyped funerary statues of other ancient rulers, these soldiers are modelled on living men. This individual portraiture of the soldiers is unique and remains unexplained. Mr Yang Chen Ching suggested that the First Emperor might have wished to celebrate the unification of China, a country of many peoples, and that is why the statues buried in the pits exhibit all the varying physical features of the inhabitants of mainland East Asia. He also argued that they not only represent the multi-racial Ch'in empire, but also bear witness to the power of the ordinary people. And the time and energy spent on the figures in the pits – the largest ones ever discovered in China – show how important they were to the First Emperor. But as one might expect, a

No two faces of the terracotta soldiers are alike; they were modelled on individual soldiers from throughout the Ch'in empire.

29

degree of standardization is apparent in the treatment of the torso. The body of each statue was manufactured separately. From the abdomen downwards the figure is solid, the weight being supported by the legs. The upper part of the body, including the head, is hollow and the forearms and hands, as well as the head, were added later. Each head is attached to the torso by an elongated cylindrical neck. Moulds must have been used, according to Mr Yang Chen Ching.

Side view of a Ch'in officer. He would have been recognized by his distinctive armour as well as by his headgear.

Individual details such as ears, beards and head decoration were then sculpted, and finally the complete statue was brightly painted. In Pit No. 1 there were probably two colour schemes for the armoured infantrymen. One group had black armour slates with white rivets, gold buttons, and purple cords. Their cloaks were green, their trousers dark blue, and their shoes black with red laces. A second group wore brown slated armour with red rivets and orange buttons

Above:
The hands and heads of the terracotta statues were the last parts to be fitted.

Below:
Rear view of the padded legs of a Ch'in soldier.

The intricate hairstyles used by the Ch'in soldiers are portrayed in detail on the terracotta figures.

Facing page:
Rear view of a Ch'in chariot horse, with beautifully combed hair.

and cords. The rest of their uniform appears to be the same as the first group, except that their shorter cloaks were red. The heads of all the statues were painted as well: the eyes were white with black irises; the eyebrows, whiskers and hair were black. Horses, not surprisingly, followed a similar pattern, with hollow bodies and solid legs. They had either brown or black coats, with white teeth and hooves, and red inside the nostrils and for the ears and mouths.

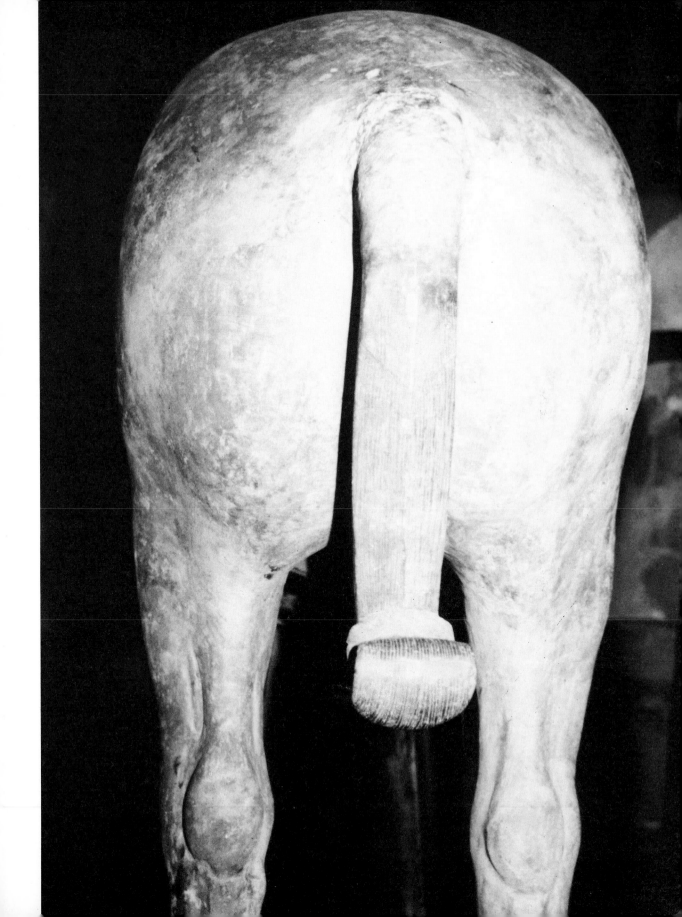

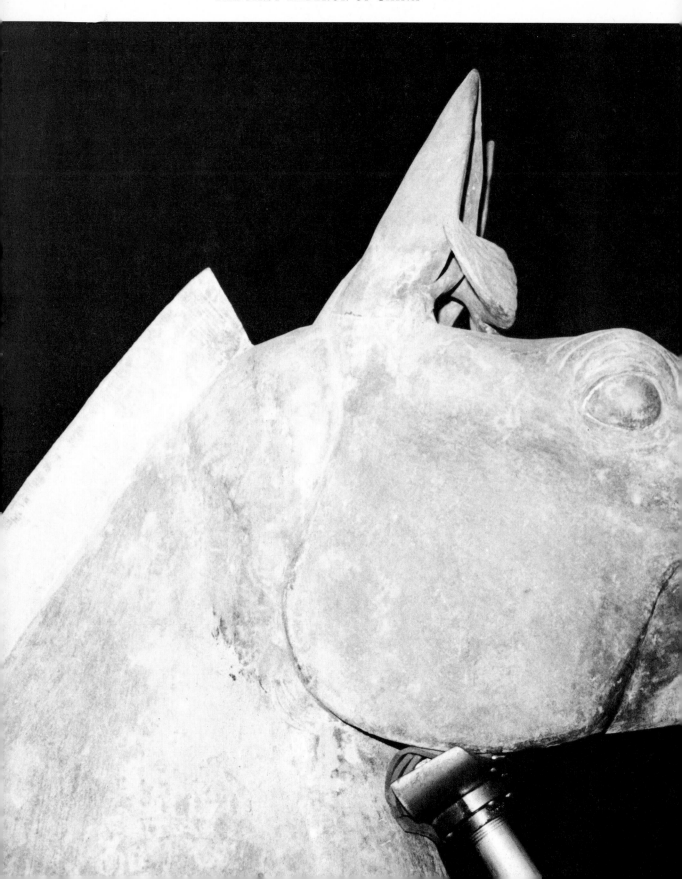

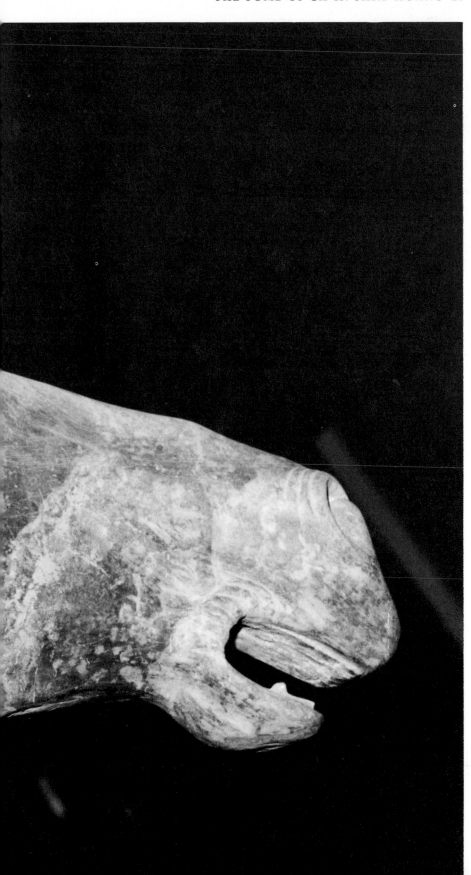

A chariot horse.
This magnificent head,
although stylized, reveals
tremendous strength in its
mouth, jaw, nostrils and
eyes.

Two small Ch'in grave-figures. The statues buried with the First Emperor, however, were life-size and individually sculptured.

At the beginning of the construction at Mount Li there were few people involved, but after 221 BC more and more labourers, totalling over half a million, were allocated to the site. It became one of the great projects of the First Emperor, equal to that of the Great Wall. In six years, only one forty-fifth of Pit No. 1 has been excavated. While Pit No. 1 is an infantry regiment, Pit No. 2 comprises a unit of war chariots and cavalry, with some unmounted support. Pit No. 3 appears to be the headquarters of the terracotta army. Pit No. 4 is empty and may never have been used at all. The second pit was discovered in May 1976 and the third a month afterwards. While the third pit has been fully explored, only a small area of the second pit has been investigated so far. At present both of them are refilled with earth. Other pits associated with the First Emperor's tomb will probably be discovered in the Mount Li area. Before the discovery of Pit No. 1 in 1974, five kneeling terracotta figures were unearthed near the outer enclosure of the mausoleum. At present there are no plans for digging the actual tomb mound. According to Mr Yang Chen Ching Pit No. 1 will take many more years; most of its statues are to be restored, leaving only a few sections to show visitors how they were found. It is the outstanding character of the site that compels its excavators to proceed slowly and carefully.

Facing page:
Pottery figure of a seated worshipper found near the tomb mound of the First Emperor in 1964. Although several of these figures were unearthed prior to the discovery of the first pit in 1974, Chinese archaeologists were surprised by the extent of the funeral preparations made by the Ch'in dynasty.

Sketchmap of a corridor of Pit No. 2. Chariots and saddle-horses with soldiers as excavated.

Pit No. 2, situated about twenty metres (sixty-six feet) north of Pit No. 1, holds slightly more than 1,400 warriors and horses divided into four groups. The construction of the second pit is similar to the first, but its more complicated layout reflects the greater variety of military personnel it contains. A projecting area at the north-eastern corner is filled by a group of kneeling armoured archers, around which stand ranks of unarmoured spearmen. Immediately behind this vanguard come two units, one essentially a mixture of chariots

Plan of Pit No. 2.

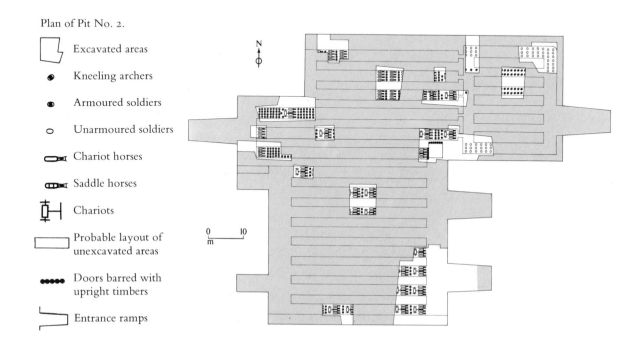

Excavated areas

Kneeling archers

Armoured soldiers

Unarmoured soldiers

Chariot horses

Saddle horses

Chariots

Probable layout of unexcavated areas

Doors barred with upright timbers

Entrance ramps

and armoured cavalry, the other chariots and armoured infantry. The fourth and largest unit consists of sixty-four chariots. In their limited excavation of this pit the Chinese have unearthed two generals, or at least two unit commanders. One stood with the infantry at the back of the vanguard, the other on a command vehicle towards the rear of the chariots and armoured infantry unit. They both wear distinctive mail coats.

  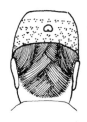

Drawings of the protective hat worn by cavalrymen.

Pit No. 3 was dug from March to December 1977. It is a small irregular chamber, about one-seventh of the area of the first pit. It was pillaged in 206 BC, but not burned by the rebels and appears to have been the place where the commander-in-chief was stationed. His war chariot is there, along with sixty-eight soldiers, many of whom are officers. The height of his guards is exceptional, being 1·9 metres (6 feet 2 inches) as opposed to an average of 1·8 metres (5 feet 9 inches) in Pit No. 1. Only the vanguard commander in the second pit is taller; he reaches 1·96 metres (6 feet 4 inches). The figure of the commander-in-chief, however, has not been discovered. There may be a connection between this fact and the huge Ch'in period tomb just fifteen metres (forty-nine feet) to the west of the third pit, though no one yet knows whether it will contain an actual interment or a terracotta statue. From the arrangement and personnel of Pit No. 3 there can be little doubt that it was the command headquarters of the pottery army. The soldiers are deployed to protect the commander-in-chief. Their armour is of two kinds: a light mail suited to rapid movement, and a heavier mail advantageous in close combat. Several of the weapons recovered had a ceremonial rather than a practical use, a fact which strengthens the argument for the importance of the third pit. Indeed, the pits can be seen as a single creation, although the fourth one is unfinished. Pit No. 3 is the controlling one for the entire 7,000-piece force. The rank of its missing commander would have

Plan of Pit No. 3.

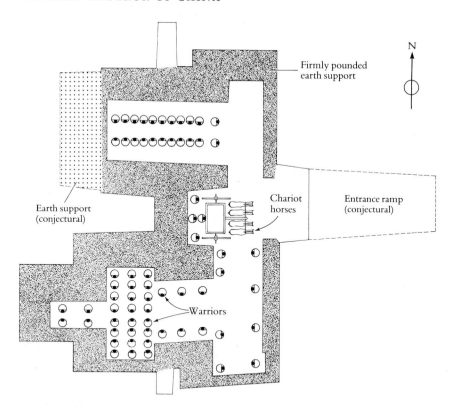

Firmly pounded
earth support

N

Earth support
(conjectural)

Chariot
horses

Entrance ramp
(conjectural)

Warriors

been a high one, at least a foremost Ch'in minister, but until further
investigations have been made, no one can be sure of his identity.

Having talked to Mr Yang Chen Ching about the enormous army
under his care, we prepared to see what it really looked like. Passing
into the heat of the Shensi afternoon, we mounted the wide steps of
the museum building, and entered through a small side entrance into
the gigantic chamber of Pit No. 1. The initial impact was unfor-
gettable. Five metres (sixteen feet) below where we stood were the
ranks of the terracotta army, a sea of faces, eyes staring hard ahead.
Although obviously static, the restored figures gave the impression
that they were poised to charge. The alertness of the crossbowmen in
the vanguard was matched by the boldness of the infantrymen
crowded behind. One was conscious of the coiled strength, the
shattering force inherent in this infantry regiment.

The Ch'in reputation on the battlefield was swiftly understood.
Here is an exact representation of the First Emperor's crack troops,
the massed columns of infantry which hurled themselves on his

Sketch layout of warriors found in Pit No. 3.

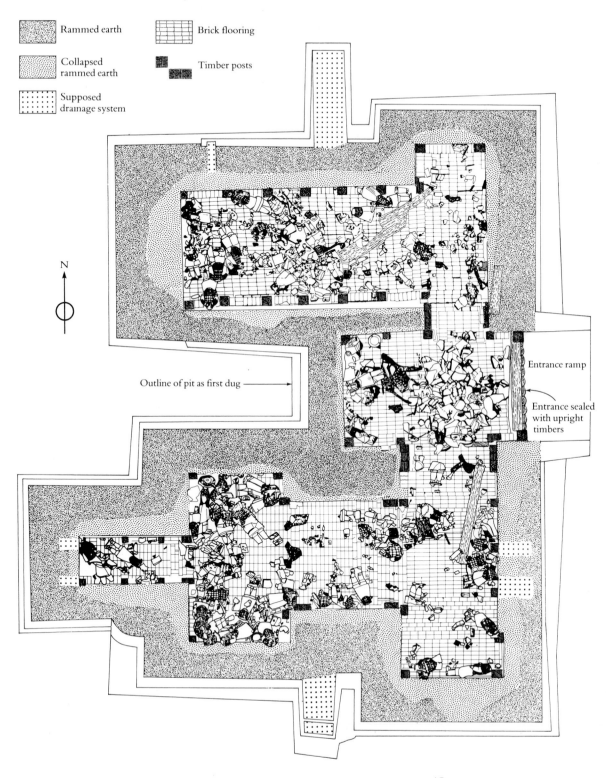

Rammed earth

Collapsed rammed earth

Supposed drainage system

Brick flooring

Timber posts

N

Outline of pit as first dug

Entrance ramp

Entrance sealed with upright timbers

The hangar-like roof over Pit No. 1 has been designed to withstand earthquakes which are a feature of the region.

enemies. Soldiers like these, and their more mobile comrades in the second pit, won the stunning victories of Ch'in in the decade before 221 BC. Their successes toppled the other feudal houses, brought about the unification of China, and placed King Cheng of Ch'in on the imperial throne. Under the command of an experienced general, these men were unbeatable. Not until the breakdown of the Ch'in empire in the reign of the Second Emperor (when violent intrigue at court and an overbearing administration in the provinces undermined its stength) did opponents arise who were capable of

overcoming the imperial forces. Even then the rebellious peasant armies had to struggle desperately hard to gain the upper hand. The hastily raised army of the tax official Chang Han, who in 208 BC recruited soldiers from the convicts actually labouring at Mount Li, crushed the first insurrection with ease. It was the intensity of popular feeling against the Ch'in dynasty coupled with the dispersal of the imperial forces in garrisons throughout the empire that gave the rebels their opportunity.

The battle-readiness of the pottery figures below us recalls Ch'in

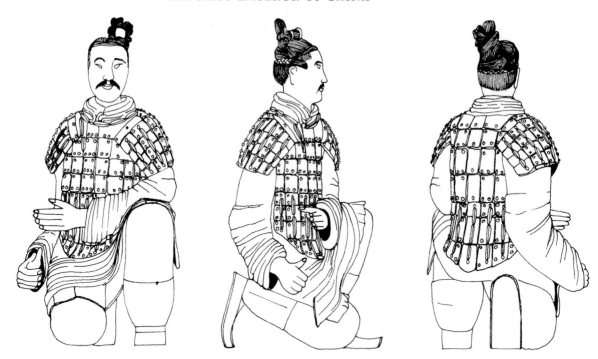

A kneeling crossbowman. Note the elaborate way in which his hair has been dressed.

might. The vanguard of archers and unarmoured spearmen, the deadlier Chinese version of the Greek peltasts, appears too nimble and vigilant for any enemy to catch the regiment off-balance. In the same way the two command vehicles and the four chariots following immediately behind the foot soldiers show how closely officered were the Ch'in armies. In *The Art of War*, Sun-tzu relates how severe the code of discipline became in the Chan Kuo period (481–221 BC).

Now gongs and drums, banners and flags are used to focus the attention of the troops. When the troops can be thus united, the brave cannot advance alone, nor can the cowardly withdraw. This is the art of employing a host. So it follows that those who when they should advance do not do so and those who when they should retire do not do so are beheaded.

When, for example, Ch'u fought against Ch'in there was an officer who before the battle was unable to control his ardour. He advanced and took a pair of heads and returned. The Ch'u general ordered his execution. Though it was pointed out how brave and talented the officer was, the general said: 'I am confident he is an officer of ability, but he is disobedient.' Thereupon he beheaded him.

Disciplined and well-trained regulars formed the nuclei of the Chan Kuo armies, and from their ranks were drawn the shock troops who spearheaded the attack in the large-scale engagements which took place right up to the triumph of Ch'in in 221 BC. It is tempting to see the pottery figures at Mount Li as a copy of an élite unit of the First Emperor's army, perhaps his equivalent of Napoleon's Imperial Guard.

Looking down at the impressive ranks of restored men, it was startling to remember that only a fraction of Pit No. 1 has been fully excavated. The corridors leading from the eastern gallery, where the vanguard is formed, have been dug for a mere twenty metres (sixty-six feet). Then there is an earthen baulk, the first of a series of baulks dividing the pit into excavation areas. Yet the cleared and restored eastern gallery and corridors are sufficient to persuade the visitor that he is privileged to gaze on a forbidden sight. We viewed the infantry regiment which the First Emperor thought he might need after death. The energy involved in preparing the terracotta army must have been enormous. Only the single-mindedness of an autocrat could have achieved these results in so short a space of time.

We noticed two artists busily drawing statues below. Although Chinese archaeologists use photography like their colleagues in other countries, they prefer to have detailed pictures from the hand of an artist specialized in copying historical objects. Mr Yang Chen Ching was evidently pleased that my son could not resist sketching the terracotta army. An official was asked to take him closer to the figures, while we moved across the site to another section. On one officer we could see the tassels representing badges of rank. Ch'in officers wore them on their armour in three places – the front, the back, and the shoulders. Soldiers could, of course, also recognise their officers by their distinctive armour. The mail coats of the two senior officers in Pit No. 2 were beautifully designed. These two generals were dressed in long suits of mail, fashioned from exceptionally smooth slates, and finished with leather tops and sleeves.

The armoured figures in the pits have confirmed the records in the histories of the elaborate defensive equipment used during the Chan Kuo period. Before the fifth century BC, armoured troops were unknown. The chariot-riding nobility engaged in archery duels, their only protection the lacquered shields carried by their retainers.

The remains of a chariot, horses and armoured infantry in Pit No. 1.

Foot soldiers had to manage with padded jackets until the introduction of garments of treated sharkskin and animal hide. War became professional only in the two centuries before the unification of China in 221 BC. It also became expensive, as larger states absorbed their smaller neighbours and diverted more and more resources to military purposes. The powerful states of Ch'in and Ch'u could each put into the field over 1,000,000 soldiers. Ch'in first broke the power of the hereditary aristocracy in the army, and promoted the brave

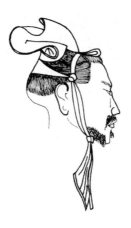

Above:
Drawings of the elaborate headwear of a general.

Centre:
Drawings of the armour of a high-ranking officer.

Below:
One of the seven kinds of armour that have been found in Pit No. 2.

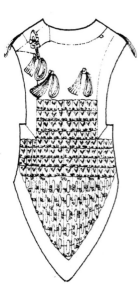
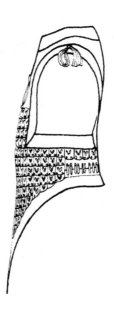
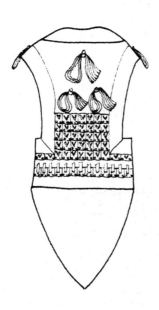

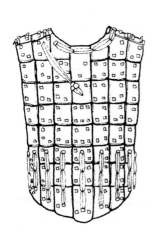

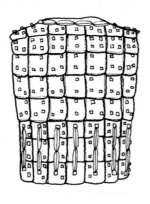

and able to the highest ranks. The ceremonial battle-axe, the symbol of the commander-in-chief, was no longer restricted to Ch'in nobles. Metal armour, the crossbow, and reliance on training had already reduced the opportunities for noble display. Pit No. 2 reveals how charioteers were obliged to fight in strict formation as part of a larger unit. They would have been as liable to punishment as anyone else, since the army was now a war machine, not a feudal host led by seasonal aristocratic generals.

In the rooms on either side of the museum forecourt are displays of archaeological finds. The blades of some weapons recovered from the pits are incredibly sharp. When they were dug up their edges were keen enough to cut a hair. They were manufactured by a unique process whereby bronze was coated with chromium. One glass cabinet contains a replica of a crossbow. The weapon is fitted with one of the bronze trigger mechanisms recovered from the pits. It looks lethal. The heavy arrows dispatched by ancient Chinese crossbowmen would have ripped straight through Greek or Macedonian shields. In present-day jargon, their firepower was unchallengeable.

Below:
An excavated sword. When it was found, it was still sharp enough to cut a hair.

Facing page above:
Spear head and crossbow bolts, unearthed from Pit No. 2.

Facing page below:
A reconstruction of a Ch'in crossbow. Bronze trigger mechanisms have been uncovered from the first, second and third pits.

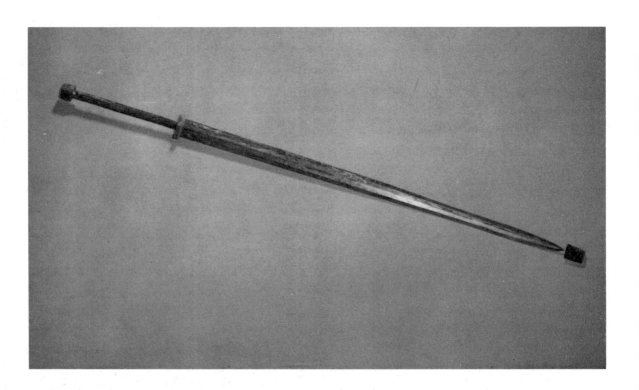

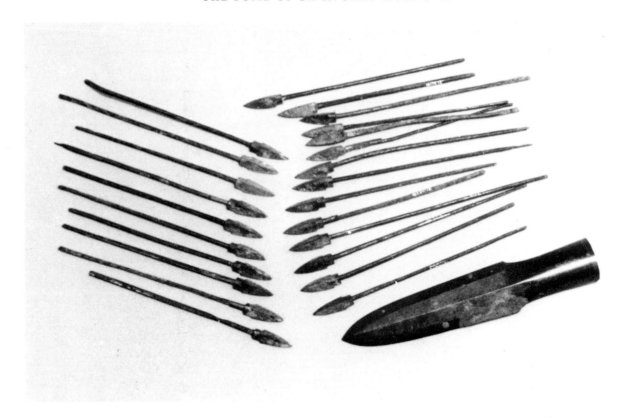

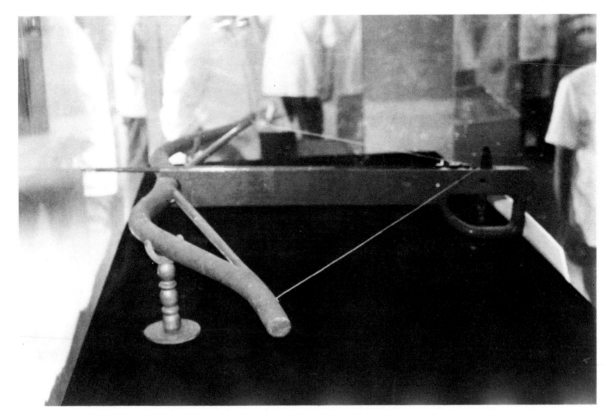

A magnificent
reproduction of a chariot
from the second pit in the
museum at Mount Li.

The headgear of a chariot driver.

We were delighted to find in an enormous glass case a reconstruction of a wooden chariot. Four magnificent terracotta horses are hitched to it by means of wooden shoulder yokes attached to a crossbar, which in turn is fixed to a central shaft. Behind the chariot itself stand two armoured men, one of whom has his arms outstretched as if he is holding the reins. All the Ch'in war chariots have a single shaft. The size of the chariot box itself ranges from 1·3 to 1·5 metres (4 feet 3 inches to 4 feet 10 inches) from front to back. Railings at the front, on the two sides, and on part of the back are about thirty centimetres (one foot) high. The wheels average 1·8 metres (5 feet 10 inches) in diameter. An unusual feature of the chariot belonging to the commander-in-chief are traces of a roof or canopy, presumably to give protection from the elements. This conveyance also has

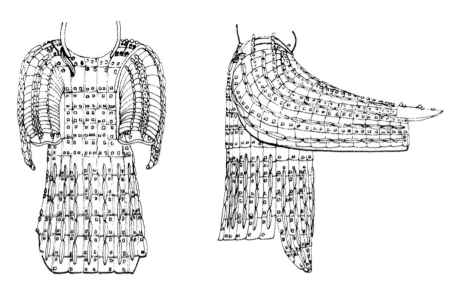

A chariot-driver's armour protected him right down to his wrists.

greater decoration than the vehicles unearthed in the first and second pits.

The mausoleum site cannot fail to go on astonishing the world over the next two decades. Surveys have already disclosed the existence of other subterranean structures, where doubtless more pottery figures will be uncovered. Unless the funerary preparations of the First Emperor were far from complete when the dynasty fell in 206 BC, there is every reason to expect that archaeologists will discover buried in the Shensi soil most of the things a great king considered indispensable in the after-life. Let us not forget that the finds at Mount Li are spread over an area equal in size to the city of Cambridge in England. There should be plenty of room for other pits, and then there remains the enigma of Ch'in Shih-huang-ti's tomb.

Chapter Two

The Land within the Passes;
Hsienyang and
the Wei river valley

In the twenty-seventh year of his reign [220 BC], Ch'in Shih-huang-ti made a tour of inspection. . . . The Hsin palace was built on the south bank of the Wei river and the First Emperor decreed that it be the Paramount Temple, representing the Apex of Heaven. From the Paramount Temple a path led to Mount Li where a front hall of the Kanchuan palace was built, and the temple was connected with Hsienyang by a walled road.

The outlying altar to the north-east of the A-fang palace platform.

This terse entry in the *Shih Chi* of Ssu-ma Ch'ien is one of many references to the First Emperor's building activities, but it is significant for us because of the cosmology implied in the imperial decree. Rarely do we have such a clear statement of religious intentions. The Paramount Temple (the site of which has still to be discovered) acted as a kind of divine marker for the grandiose works commissioned to the south of Hsienyang, the Ch'in capital. In the mind of the First Emperor the temples, palaces, gardens, and tomb he ordered to be erected were doubtless envisaged as a whole. Besides giving expression to the greatness of his reign as the very first ruler of all China, these magnificent projects would have been laid out according to a definite plan and one in which cosmic alignment received proper attention.

South of Hsienyang today are the remains of another impressive monument – the immense earthen base of the A-fang palace. The surviving portions are now cultivated or covered in wild grasses or trees. On the July day when we turned off the Sian–Hsienyang road to visit them, there was not a cloud in the sky. Our driver took us down bumpy country lanes, past the rammed-earth walls of village compounds, and eventually stopped near an outlying mound. Situated to the north-east of the main earthen base of the palace, this twenty-metre (sixty-six-foot) high hillock is thought to have served as an altar for imperial offerings. From the top we could observe the diligence of the peasant farmer, his expert use of irrigation and fertilizer, and could not fail to appreciate the traditions of intensive agriculture long established here in the Wei river valley. The wealth

The outline of A-fang palace with its altar mound to the north-east.

Local girls resting on the top of the altar mound.

of Ch'in derived from the rich soil of its heartland, the Land within the Passes, an area pre-eminently suited to large-scale water-conservancy schemes. The re-siting of the Ch'in capital at Hsienyang in 350 BC was in part due to a recognition of the crucial role agriculture played in maintaining the independence of the state.

Nothing the First Emperor did was done half-heartedly. The A-fang palace, like the Great Wall itself, was destined for legendary fame as soon as he conceived the idea of having a new residence constructed. Ssu-ma Ch'ien recounts that

> *in the thirty-fifth year of the First Emperor's reign [212 BC] a road was built through Chiu-yang to Yunyang. In order to make it straight hills were levelled and valleys filled.*
>
> *The First Emperor said: 'Hsienyang is overcrowded and the palaces of the former kings are too small. I have heard that King Wen of Chou had his capital at Feng, King Wu at Hao. The area between Feng and Hao is fit for an imperial residence.'*
>
> *Then he had palaces constructed in the Shanglin gardens, south of the Wei river. The front palace, A-fang, was built first; its measurements were 500 paces from east to west, and 500 paces from north to south. The terraces above could seat 10,000, and below there was room for banners twenty metres [sixty-six feet] in height. One causeway round the palace led to the South Hill at the top of which a gateway was erected. A second led across the Wei river to Hsienyang, just as the Heavenly Corridor in the sky leads from the Apex of Heaven across the Milky Way to the Royal Chamber. Before the completion of this palace, the First Emperor wished to choose a good name for it. But because of its closeness to old palaces, it was commonly called A-fang, meaning beside the palace. More than 700,000 workers – men punished by castration or sentenced to penal servitude – were drafted to build the A-fang palace and the emperor's tomb on Mount Li. Stone was quarried from the northern hills, timber brought from Shu and Ch'u. Three hundred palaces were built within the Pass, and east of it more than four hundred.*

But the A-fang palace, like the funerary arrangements at Mount Li, was still incomplete at the time of the First Emperor's death.

Besides the outline of the massive earthen base that one could see to the west of our vantage point on the altar mound, there are few

The main base platform of the A-fang palace. In Chinese history, this building represents untold luxury and waste.

material remains of the huge palace complex that was once under construction here. The Shensi Provincial Museum in Sian houses most of the finds. They comprise pieces of the palace roof and walls: damaged tile ends, melted bronze ornaments, and broken iron clamps. In their cases, the shattered and charred A-fang exhibits look rather forlorn. A similar atmosphere surrounds the actual palace site itself, as if the rebellious peasants who overthrew the Ch'in dynasty and razed these buildings to the ground were giving notice of the fragility of kingship.

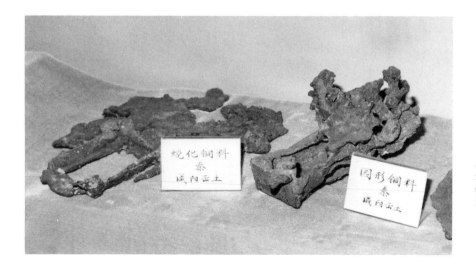

A piece of charred bronze from the A-fang palace in the Shensi Provincial Museum.

The size of the A-fang palace was extraordinary, beyond anything known in Chinese history. But then so was that of the Great Wall, a defensive work built against the northern nomads and measuring over 3,000 kilometres (1,864 miles) in length. Such extensive construction and engineering projects not only required huge amounts of manpower but also necessitated the assembly and transport of large quantities of building materials, thus imposing a heavy burden on the ordinary people. In the same way, the continual use of enforced labour throughout the empire had strained the allegiance of the peasantry, especially when it was maintained by the naked force of cruel punishments. After the death of the First Emperor in 210 BC, the Second Emperor stepped up this practice by conscripting the poorest peasants living to the 'left of the gate' for prolonged periods of military duties in outlying territories. As a result of this expansion of state demand for manpower it would seem that there was a drop in agricultural output, with all the miseries that a shortage of food entails. It was the dislocation of the rural economy that formed the background for the popular uprisings against the house of Ch'in. The landless peasants who in 209 BC led the first large-scale peasant rebellion in Chinese history were unconsciously responding to the unique circumstances of a unified empire: they were marking the limits of future authority for a centralized government.

Our visit to A-fang over, we continued to Hsienyang. We were fortunate to have permission to go to the Hsienyang Municipal Museum, because it is still in the process of being organized. Hsienyang is now a well-equipped industrial town and important textile centre. Before the founding of the People's Republic, the cotton crop of Shensi was transported to the textile ports on the coast, an expensive and cumbersome journey. Passing over the new Wei river bridge, we observed the majestic sweep of this river, slow and low in the heat of summer. The water channel was close to the Hsienyang bank, while elsewhere on the river bed small groups of workmen were sieving the dry silt. In China nothing is wasted. We turned off the main road immediately after reaching the other side of the bridge, and a series of narrow streets brought us to the museum, which like many others today is housed in a Confucian temple. A magnificent ornamental gateway acts as the entrance, its overhanging brackets and runners resplendent in the hot sun. We were told by a member of the museum staff that the red, green, white, and blue paint had been freshly lacquered for the forthcoming official opening.

Over a cup of tea, we discussed with staff members the rooms of exhibits being prepared for display. They informed us that people kept finding ancient artefacts. Hardly a month goes by without the discovery of an important object. They come not only from the ruins of the Ch'in capital, but from the whole area north of the Wei river, which was favoured for burial during the Han and T'ang dynasties. There are, for instance, the tombs of five Han emperors in the foothills behind the town. The museum is rich in archaeological finds of the Ch'in, Han and T'ang periods.

Ancient Hsienyang, the capital of the First Emperor, was the last Ch'in capital. The Ch'in people moved down the course of the Wei river to this site over several centuries. They appear first in the province of Kansu, reaching the province of Shensi only in the eighth

Overleaf:
View of the Wei river from the Hsienyang city bridge. Irrigation in this region established Ch'in as the pre-eminent feudal state prior to the unification of China in 221 BC.

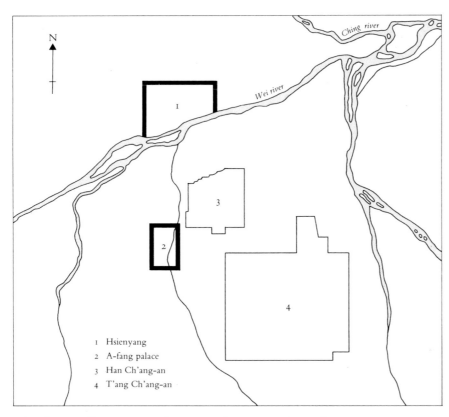

Sketchmap of Sian area, showing relative positions of Ch'in, Han and T'ang dynasty foundations

century BC. About 140 kilometres (87 miles) west of Hsienyang are the remains of three early capitals, the most important of which was Yong, a site occupied from 667 to 384 BC. This settlement possessed an enclosing wall, like all ancient Chinese cities. In 383 BC the capital was again moved nearly 170 kilometres (106 miles) downstream to Yuyang, east of Hsienyang. At Yuyang there are traces of a rammed-earth city wall nearly two kilometres (three-quarters of a mile) square as well as north–south and east–west thoroughfares, workshops, wells, and a system of public drainage. It was in 350 BC that the present site of Hsienyang was selected as the capital. Between that date and its destruction in 206 BC the city acted as the administrative centre of first a powerful feudal state, then of a unified empire which included all of ancient China. After 221 BC Hsienyang was the country's political, economic and cultural powerhouse. To ensure the capital was without rival 120,000 aristocratic and wealthy families were forcibly resettled here. This concentration of wealth and talent alone would have transformed Hsienyang into the premier city in China. The First Emperor ordered the most extensive building programme recorded in Chinese history and he drew to Hsienyang craftsmen and artisans from all over the empire.

Although the nobles were an ornament to the capital and stimulated its embellishment, the political motive behind the First Emperor's action was their effective separation from the feudal lands and followers he had abolished. Ssu-ma Ch'ien says in the *Shih Chi*:

> 120,000 *wealthy families were brought from all over the empire to Hsienyang. The imperial ancestral temples, the Changtai palace, and the Shanglin gardens were constructed on the south bank of the Wei river. Each time Ch'in had conquered a feudal state, a replica of its ruler's palace was rebuilt on the hills north of the capital overlooking the Wei river to the south. These palaces covered the area from Yungmen to the Ching and Wei rivers. Connected by elevated avenues and courts with pavilions, they were filled with the beautiful women and instruments captured from the different states.*

The policy of concentration, known as 'to strengthen the trunk and weaken the branches', was used by later dynasties as a method of controlling local separatism, but no ruler ever equalled the First

Emperor's determined drive against feudalism. His resoluteness encompassed even the imperial family, as none of the princes were enfeoffed. The First Emperor was almost certainly guided in this matter by his prime minister, Li Ssu (*c.* 280–208 BC).

The northerly movement of the Wei river has destroyed much of the ancient city of Hsienyang. However, the rebels in 206 BC mercilessly sacked it. The histories tell us that the Ch'in capital burned for three months and, as wood was the chief building material employed, the ruin would have been complete. So far, archaeological investigations have brought to light two sites dating from the reign of the First Emperor. The first, in the north-eastern part of modern Hsienyang, reveals segments of rammed-earth walls and remains of substantial houses built on earthen platforms. In one of the residences there are traces of plaster and a fresco on the walls. Bronze vessels, iron nails, clay tiles, and bone artefacts abound, as do pipes made from thick stoneware. The clay pipes probably once formed the water-conduits in an ancient network of underground drainage. There are also wells, pottery kilns and storage pits. The second site, to the south-east of the first one, may well include the replica palaces that the First Emperor ordered to be constructed whenever he toppled a rival monarch. Spread over an area some twelve kilometres (seven miles) from east to west are numerous rammed-earth foundations. In the Hsienyang museum there is a tentative reconstruction of one of the large buildings they supported. It is a three-storey structure, with elevated corridors, a built-in heating system, and a network of subterranean drains. In its day this palace would have been brightly decorated.

We moved on to look at the rooms containing the Ch'in exhibits. Passing through the first courtyard of the old temple, the colonnaded buildings on each side presented to us a cheerful row of red pillars. The first room is closest to the front entrance of the museum and when the building was a Confucian temple, it would have acted as the reception hall for worshippers. Now the big room is filled with glass cases, though one of Confucius' sayings, 'Scrutinize your own heart three times a day', remains on a wall. A bronze bell, the sort used by ancient Chinese armies for signalling a retreat immediately caught our eye. The command vehicles in the pottery army at Mount Li would have been equipped with such instruments.

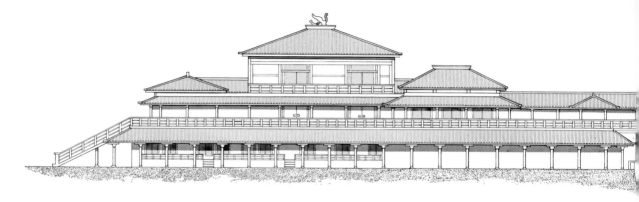

A drawing of Ch'in arms. From top to bottom, three spears, two halberds and a sword. The halberd was a favourite weapon.

Officers would have indicated that an advance was necessary through the beating of a drum. This particular bronze bell is beautifully cast, with intricate cloud patterns on its sides and a tiger standing fiercely on the top. Chinese bells do not have an internal clapper; they are always struck from the outside, like the gong. Near by are other

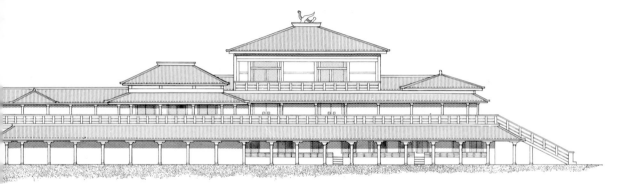

Drawing of a Ch'in palace in Hsienyang.

exhibits of a warlike character – bronze swords, daggers, spear heads, arrow points, halberds, and crossbow triggers. Here is an example of the short, wide-bladed sword carried by Ch'in foot soldiers. Around the handle are moulded two rings so as to allow the fingers a firmer grip. Next to it lies a halberd, that lethal combination of spear and battle-axe. The Ch'in halberd was tied on to the end of a shaft, probably a length of bamboo, and protruded to one side by as much as forty centimetres (fifteen inches). It would have been a dangerous weapon in the hands of a Ch'in infantryman, who specialized in the tumult of hand-to-hand combat. Judging from extant remains the metal favoured in Ch'in weaponry appears to have been bronze, and not iron as some historians have thought. Further excavation may justify those who argue that the shattering victories of Ch'in over the other feudal states were achieved by means of low-grade steel weapons, but at the moment there is no archaeological evidence.

The short, wide-bladed swords carried by Ch'in foot soldiers.

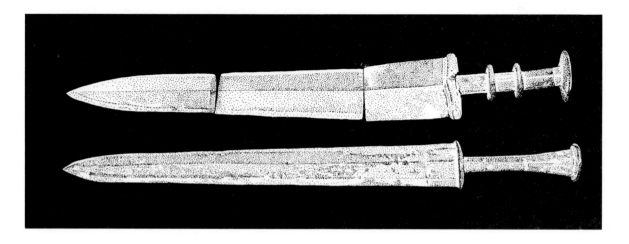

One of the standard
weights introduced
throughout China under
the Ch'in empire.

A liquid container in the
form of a ram. Found in
Hsienyang in the 1970s,
this piece of pottery set off
a major excavation of the
north-eastern part of the
city.

From the *Chan-kuo Ts'e (Intrigues of the Warring States)* – in which are recounted stories of political rivalry between about 300 and 221 BC – we are made aware of Ch'in military might. It records a pertinent interview with King Chao-hsiang, whose long reign from 306 to 251 BC witnessed the apparently inexorable rise of the Ch'in state. Seeking to persuade King Chao-hsiang to dominate the middle Yellow river valley by overrunning the small states of Wei and Han, an adviser says:

> *Your majesty's country has Kan-ch'uan and Ku-k'ou in the north, the rivers Ching and Wei girdling its south, with Lung and Shu to the right and chasms and slopes to the left. With a thousand war chariots and a million crack troops – taking into account the bravery of Ch'in's infantry and the multitude of her riders – if you should go against the other feudal lords it would be like letting slip the hound against a crippled hare, your supremacy would be established at once. But instead of this you close your passes and fear even to let your forces peer in China east of the mountains.*

The strength of the natural defences of the Land within the Passes and the boldness of the armoured foot soldiers, the ancestors of the pottery regiment buried at Mount Li, are being advanced as reasons for action. Underlying the military capacity, however, was an agricultural revolution which only reached its fruition during the reign of King Cheng, the future First Emperor. A considerable number of the surviving Ch'in exhibits reflect this agricultural prosperity. A clay model of a silo recalls the care taken by the authorities in storing the abundant harvests. Quite charming, too, is a jar shaped as a kneeling ram, a container for liquid probably once in the possession of a well-to-do Ch'in household. A small handle rises conveniently from its back. The commonest design for wine or liquid storage vessels is a flattened gourd, with a small neck and a strengthened mouth.

In another room of the museum we were shown relics from the palace quarter of ancient Hsienyang. There are broken *wa-t'ang*, the circular ends of tiles used along the edges of roofs. These are decorated with a variety of stylized patterns based on animals, insects, vegetables and clouds. There are motifs derived from frogs, birds, dragonflies, cicadas and butterflies. No less extravagant are the

Model of a grain silo found in Hsienyang. It indicates the care taken by the Ch'in authorities in agricultural matters.

impressed and incised bricks on display. One large brick has had a swirling dragon cut along its edge; the eyes of the creature stare out haughtily because in Chinese myth the *lung*, or dragon, is essentially a benevolent divinity and held in high regard. He is the rain-bringer, the lord of waters, clouds, rivers, marshes, lakes and seas. Extremely versatile, he can make himself as tiny as a silkworm or become so big that he can overshadow the whole world. He can soar through the clouds as well as penetrate the deepest springs. His appearance is made up of the horns of a stag, the head of a camel, the eyes of a demon, the scales of a fish, the claws of an eagle, the pads of a tiger, the ears of a bull, and the long whiskers of a cat. Although dragons were always traditionally associated with the Chinese emperor, it is likely that for the First Emperor these potent divinities had an even more special appeal, and therefore were accorded a prominent place in official iconography. Other decorative symbols emphasizing the supernatural right of the First Emperor to universal authority were the phoenix, long a harbinger of peace as well as good fortune, and the lightning cloud.

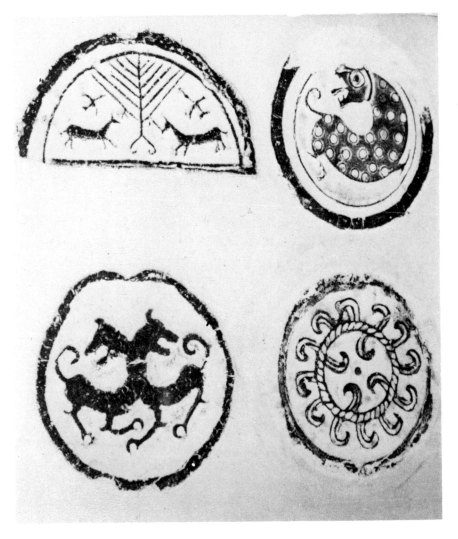

Wa-t'angs are circular tile-ends and have been unearthed from a palace building in Hsienyang. They are decorated with a variety of stylized patterns based on animals, insects, vegetables and clouds.

Left:
An incised brick from
Hsienyang, showing a
man riding a phoenix,
and, *above*, a dragon.

Right:
An impressed brick
showing animals pursued
by mounted huntsmen,
excavated in 1957.

Below:
A drawing of the
refrigerator found in
Hsienyang.

Bricks decorated with more conventional designs have been unearthed from several sites in the Wei river valley. In 1957 at Mount Li a brick was found impressed with a hunting scene in which mounted archers gave chase to deer. This may well recall the imperial hunts in the Shanglin gardens, the enormous open space across the river from Hsienyang where the First Emperor had the A-fang palace built. However, the luxury of the capital is perhaps best represented in the remnants of a refrigerator which consists of a number of terracotta rings, approximately one metre (three feet) high and 1·75 metres (5 feet 8 inches) in diameter, sunk thirteen metres (forty-three feet) into the ground to serve as a cold storage pit.

At both the Shensi Provincial Museum and the Hsienyang Municipal Museum there are many examples of the reforming zeal of the First Emperor in the guise of standard weights and measures. An inscription on one oval iron weight of 32 kilograms (71 pounds) reads:

In the twenty-sixth year of his reign [221 BC], Ch'in Shih-huang-ti annexed all the feudal lands under Heaven, brought peace to the black-headed people, and proclaimed himself sole ruler. Then, he issued a decree to his ministers, ordering them to clarify and unify all laws and weights and measures which were perplexing or were not uniform.

This brief inscription of forty characters is evidence of the all-embracing nature of the Ch'in reformation of ancient China. Weights and measures, coinage, transport – every aspect of daily affairs came under state scrutiny and regulation. While there must have been a pressing need to sort out the muddle of precepts and customs inherited from the various feudal states, Ssu-ma Ch'ien suggests that the First Emperor's anxiety about orderliness and uniformity arose from his belief in 'the Five Elements'. The *Shih Chi* devotes an entire paragraph to the subject.

Ch'in Shih-huang-ti advanced the theory of the cyclic revolution of the Five Elements. He believed that the authority of Chou had been supplanted by that of Ch'in because Ch'in's element was water and Chou's fire. So began the era of the Power of Water. The start of the year was changed to the first day of the tenth month, when a court celebration was held. Black became the chief colour for dress, banners and pennants, and six the chief number. Tallies and official headgear were six 'inches' long, carriages six 'feet' wide, one pace was six 'feet', and the imperial carriage had six horses. Ch'in Shih-huang-ti renamed the Yellow River the Powerful Water. In order to inaugurate the Power of Water it was believed that there must be firm repression with everything determined by law. Only ruthless, implacable severity could make the Five Elements accord. So the law was harsh and there were no amnesties.

Facing page above:
A pottery measure. Strict standardization of weights and measures throughout his empire was one of Ch'in Shih-huang-ti's aims.

Below:
The script from this pottery measure, found in Shantung in 1963.

The effects of the First Emperor's belief extended to his characteristic thoroughness in dealing with matters of policy.

'Correctness' in everything was rigidly enforced after unification, as shown by quantities of pottery measures turning up in the Land within the Passes and outside. One, which was excavated on the peninsula of Shantung in 1963, actually refers to the priority placed by the First Emperor on 'reducing all in a uniform manner'. It also appears that many of the convicts who laboured on the A-fang palace and the Mount Li mausoleum had been sentenced for disregarding standard weights and measures.

On the road back to Sian from Hsienyang the natural advantages of the Land within the Passes could be observed. This is loess country. Thick deposits of windblown yellow earth, varying from thirty to one hundred metres (98 to 328 feet), cover the landscape. The fine soil originated from the Mongolian plateau at the time when it was well watered and fertile. Changes in climate, brought about by the Ice Age and the uplift of the Tibetan plateau which cut off the monsoon rains from the Indian Ocean, reduced the earth to a fine dust which was carried southwards by the cold winds. Present-day dust storms are but a gentler continuation of this age-old geological process. The very nature of the loess soil inaugurated what was to be the foundation of Chinese civilization: it encouraged the development of water control. The Ch'in rulers in particular undertook large-scale conservancy schemes, notably the Chengkuo canal opened in 246 BC, to make the countryside safe from floods and well irrigated for agriculture. Because loess soil is so fine it retains moisture easily and by a capillary action draws to the roots of crops minerals hidden deep below. Loess is a self-fertilizing sponge. All that is required for bumper harvests is an adequate supply of water, which the erratic rainfall in the Wei river valley cannot provide. Looking now at the green lines of maize stretched out as far as the eye could see on either side of the road, we could appreciate the effect on agricultural productivity that the Chengkuo canal must have had. The *Shih Chi* tells us that this project, to the north of Hsienyang, transformed poor land into 'a fertile plain without bad years'. The future First Emperor, therefore, found himself in receipt of more grain tax than any of his feudal rivals, a supply so vast and sure that he could launch campaigns at any moment he chose, without fear that a massive call-up of his farmer-soldiers would lead to crop failure and famine. None could stand against his forces. No army could strike at his stronghold. The Land within the Passes and its satellite territory of Shu-Pa in modern Szechuan are the two most nearly impregnable natural sanctuaries in China, well insulated from the east and south by mountains and gorges. It seemed in 221 BC when the First Emperor assumed the imperial title that his house would last 'for endless generations'. That spirit of confidence is manifest in the inscription he had had carved two years later.

In the twenty-eighth year of his reign
A new age is opened by Ch'in Shih-huang-ti.
Rules and measures are corrected,
Everything is set in order,
Human affairs are clarified
And there is harmony between fathers and sons.
Ch'in Shih-huang-ti in his wisdom, benevolence and justice
Has made all laws and principles clear.
He set forth to pacify the east,
To inspect officers and men.
This long tour over,
He visited the coast.
Great are the Sovereign's achievements.

Facing page:
The might of the Ch'in army is illustrated by the vivid details on the faces of the terracotta army.

Men attend diligently to basic tasks,
Farming is encouraged, not secondary pursuits;
All the ordinary people prosper.
All men under Heaven
Toil with a common purpose.
Tools and measures are the same,
The written script is standardized.
Wherever the sun and moon shine.
Wherever one can go by boat or by carriage,
Men obey their orders
And satisfy their desires.
For our Sovereign in accordance with the time
Has regulated local customs,
Constructed waterways and divided up the land.
Caring for the ordinary people,
He works day and night without rest;
He defines the laws leaving none in doubt,
Making known what is forbidden.
The local officials have their duties,
Administration is smoothly carried out,
All is done correctly, all according to plan.
Ch'in Shih-huang-ti in his wisdom
Inspects all four quarters of his realm.
High and low, noble and humble,
None dare overshoot the mark;
No evil or impropriety is tolerated,
So all strive to be excellent men
And exert themselves in tasks great and small;
None dare to idle or ignore their duties,
But in far-off, remote places
Serious and decorous administrators
Work steadily, loyal and just.
Great is the virtue of our Sovereign
Who pacifies all under Heaven,
Who punishes traitors, exterminates evil men,
And with apt measures brings prosperity.
Tasks are done in their proper season,
All things flourish and grow.

The ordinary people know peace,
Having laid aside weapons and armour;
Kinsmen help each other,
There are no robbers or thieves;
Men delight in his rule,
All understanding law and discipline.
The whole universe
Is Ch'in Shih-huang-ti's realm,
Extending west to the desert,
South to where the houses face north,
East to the ocean there,
North to beyond Ta-hsia;
Wherever life is found,
All acknowledge his suzerainty,
His achievements surpass those of the Five Emperors,
His kindness reaches even to the beasts of the field;
All creatures benefit from his virtue,
All live in peace at home.

Even allowing for the fulsome flattery of the official style, with its inevitable references to the virtue of the monarch and the gratitude of his subjects, the list of achievements is impressive. The triumph of Ch'in was not simply a tale of military decisiveness sweeping away the anarchy of decayed feudalism. Unification under the First Emperor subsumed processes long at work in ancient Chinese society. It was the First Emperor's historical role to be the country's first unifier. His vigour and ruthlessness were obviously crucial in hastening the demise of feudalism, just as they were responsible for the upsurge of popular rebellions after his death, but above all the system of government that he founded was to prove invaluable to the Chinese. Though the Ch'in dynasty soon passed into oblivion, the imperial system itself endured for very many generations indeed.

PART TWO

THE
HISTORICAL
CONTEXT

Chapter Three

Feudal Decline; the Ch'un Ch'iu period, 770-481 BC

The start of the decline of feudalism and the movement towards unity can be discerned in the Ch'un Ch'iu or Spring and Autumn period (770–481 BC), called after annals of the same name. It is here that we find the hereditary principle first challenged.

Chinese feudalism had reached its highest point during the Western Chou period (1027–771 BC). The Chou people, who were half nomadic and half agricultural a generation or so before their ascendancy, overthrew between 1122 and 1027 BC, the Shang, the earliest dynasty attested to by archaeology. Following the destruction of Anyang, the last Shang capital, these aggressive westerners assumed dominance of northern China. Although their relative backwardness may have inclined the Chou to adopt the existing structure of the Shang state – their early bronzes seem less fine than those of the late Shang – in their subjugation of the populous eastern plain they brought the feudal system to full maturity. Chou princes and royal kinsmen were installed as lords of the lower reaches of the Yellow river, their authority initially maintained by garrisons of Chou warriors. These vassals owed allegiance to the Chou king, who was also looked upon as a religious leader. As *t'ien tzu*, the Son of Heaven, he acted as chief worshipper in the state ancestral cult, claiming his own line of descent from the supreme deity and founder-ancestor of the Chou people. The goodwill of Shang Ti, the heavenly power, had definite political implications, since the unworthiness of a monarch would be revealed in natural phenomena. The *Shu Ching* (*Book of Documents*), tells us how 'the earth shook' and 'the rivers dried up' before the fall of the last Shang king.

The extension of Chou power into the lower Yellow river valley eventually led to the formation of the feudal states. As time passed, local hostility to the Chou nobles decreased and their kinship ties with the homeland, situated in the Wei river valley like later Ch'in, became attenuated. Retainers were no longer drawn exclusively from the Chou people. Nor was the military strength of the Chou king secure even along the Wei river. In 771 BC, the capital of Hao was sacked as a result of an alliance between barbarian tribesmen and relations of the queen, who had been set aside because of the ruler's infatuation with a favourite concubine. The house of Chou recovered from this catastrophe, though a new capital had to be established in a safer place at Loyang, far downstream. Royal authority was severely diminished and power transferred to those nobles who held great fiefs. In 707 BC the royal army was even defeated by a force from Cheng, a territory previously under Chou suzerainty.

The *Shu Ching* offers an insight into the reduced circumstances of the Son of Heaven, the One Man, after the nobles had rallied against the barbarian invaders in 771 BC. The nobles declared the heir to the throne their overlord, and this young prince, known as King P'ing, addressed his chief benefactor in the following terms:

Uncle I Ho, how illustrious were (our first kings)! Their brilliant virtue rose brightly on high and the fame of it was renowned here below. Therefore Heaven favoured them . . . There were ministers who aided and illustriously served their sovereigns, following and carrying out their plans, both great and small, so that my fathers sat tranquilly on the throne.

Oh! What an object of pity am I, a mere Child. Just as I am enthroned, Heaven has severely chastised me. Because of the lack of royal beneficence . . . the barbarous tribes of the west have savaged our kingdom. Furthermore, among my ministers there are none of age and experience and distinguished ability in their offices. I am thus unequal to the difficulties of my position and I hope that my granduncles and uncles will show compassion towards me. If only there were those who could establish their merit on behalf of me, the One Man, then I might long enjoy peace on the throne.

King P'ing goes on to ask his relative to return to his lands and restore order. A gift of a bow and one hundred arrows indicates the ruler's concern, for it represented the authority to punish any who were disobedient to royal commands. In this passage the Chou king openly admits his dependence on his peers. In the Ch'un Ch'iu period this central weakness became apparent to all: the great lords controlled states independent in all but name.

The nobles, *de facto* rulers of their own territories, possessed various titles. Beneath the Son of Heaven there were four ranks: *kung*, duke; *hou*, marquis; *po*, earl; *tsu*, viscount, and *nan*, baron, each of equal dignity. These titles, however, did not accurately reflect status, because the heads of the feudal states were at first considered to be equal. According to the *Li Chi* (*Record of Rites*), a total of 1,763 fiefs existed during the Western Chou period. The number is probably exaggerated, but the over-elaboration of feudalism under Chou, together with a complete lack of any means, beyond kinship and morality, of holding the system together, does explain the extent of the political breakdown after 771 BC. Later, Li Ssu, the First Emperor's chief adviser, was convinced that he knew where the blame had lain. Dissuading Ch'in Shih-huang-ti from investing 'the sons of the imperial family' with territories, he argued in 221 BC that 'the fiefs given by the kings of Chou to their sons, younger brothers and members of their family, were extremely numerous. But as time passed these near relatives became divided and estranged; they attacked each other as if they were enemies. More and more the feudal lords killed and warred with one another, without the Son of Heaven of Chou being able to prevent them.'

Like the Chou king himself, each territorial magnate set up his own ancestral temple in the fortified city where he had his seat. Like the king, he installed his brothers in dominant positions and distributed lands within his own state to loyal ministers, senior officials and leading soldiers in his service. At the outset of the Ch'un Ch'iu period, the 'state' was little more than an enlarged household. There were two ranks of ministers, the *ch'ing* and the *tai fu*: the former tended to be the preserve of the feudal house, the few close relations holding senior posts, while the latter supplied opportunities of advancement for less well-connected families. The feudal lord and his aristocratic ministers of various grades constituted the power group in the state. Between this élite and the people was a knightly class, the *shih*, whose forefathers were high officials or even feudal dignitaries.

The *shih* received the same training as their superiors, namely the Six Skills; propriety of conduct, music, archery, chariot driving, writing and arithmetic. They might be small landlords, minor government officials, followers of powerful families, or even farmers. The growth of this class after 771 BC, a consequence of the blurring of feudal distinctions and the disappearance of many states, altered the balance of Chinese society. In the teachings of Confucius (551–479 BC) the pride and loyalty of the *shih* were to be elevated into moral attributes, making up the essential character of an educated man. The family of Confucius was certainly *shih*, and it may have descended from the royal house of Shang. This ancestry may partly explain why the philosopher always strove for reform and justice within the framework of feudalism.

Everything depended on the toil of the people, the *nung* or peasant farmers. Their work was considered productive and fundamental, for it sustained society. The work of the few artisans (*kung*) and merchants (*shang*) was looked upon as non-productive and secondary. In the early Ch'un Ch'iu period trade had hardly developed. The aristocrats, provided by the *nung* with food, clothing and labour, wanted only a few commodities, such as jewellery and salt, from outside their lands. It was said that 'Lords live on tribute, ministers on their estates, *shih* on the land, and peasants on their own toil.' The ideal life of the peasant is depicted in the *Shih Ching*, or *Book of Poetry*. This verse describes some of the services rendered by the *nung*:

> *In the fourth month the milkwort is in spike,*
> *In the fifth month the cicada cries.*
> *In the eighth month the harvest is gathered,*
> *In the tenth month the bough falls.*
> *In the days of the First we hunt the racoon,*
> *And take those foxes and wild-cats*
> *To make furs for our Lord.*
> *In the days of the Second is the great Meet;*
> *Practice for deeds of war.*
> *The one-year-old boar we keep;*
> *The three-year-old we offer to our Lord.*

The picture given is one of peace and prosperity, of an orderly rural life, and cordial relations between noble and peasant, but there can be little doubt that life was hard for the tillers of the soil. They had to work from dawn to dusk and were at the beck and call of their masters. They were also bound to the land and transferred with it from one landlord to another. However, the essential importance of agriculture to Chinese civilization was fully recognized by the nobility and the welfare of the peasant farmers was achieved by the construction of mud-walled villages that afforded winter shelter as well as protection from marauders. Permanent fields had replaced the primitive system of burn-and-clear agriculture and in 594 BC the state of Lu levied the first land tax of which there is a record.

By 700 BC Chou had sunk to the level of its former vassals, though nominally it still ruled over China. The Chou king retained undisputed only a religious function in the small and impoverished royal domain surrounding Loyang. The resulting power vacuum was imperfectly filled by the hegemon system. The first overlord (*pa*) was Duke Huan of Ch'i, a prosperous state straddling the mouth of the Yellow river and bordering on the northeastern seaboard. Ch'i's economic superiority derived from its monopoly of salt and its efficient use of land. Significantly Duke Huan (ruled 685–643 BC) is credited with the building of dikes along the lower reaches of the Yellow river, thereby concentrating the nine streams of the previous delta into one. This early experiment of hydraulic engineering failed but large-scale irrigation and flood-control schemes were later to become standard features of policy among the feudal states.

As the first hegemon, Duke Huan attempted to maintain the peace and repel barbarian inroads. Conferences were called to discuss points of mutual interest, such as the sharing of rivers, and alliances were formed against truculent states such as semi-barbarian Ch'u in the south. Mencius (*c.* 390–305 BC), Confucius' most famous follower, records the terms of an agreement signed at the end of a conference. Signatories are charged with punishing the unfilial, defending the principle of inheritance, honouring the worthy, respecting the aged, protecting children and strangers, choosing talented officials instead of relying on hereditary offices, abstaining from putting great officials to death, and avoiding acts of provocation, such as the construction of barriers, the unannounced placing of boundary markers, and the restriction of the sale of grain.

A semblance of order was thus maintained. Duke Huan, ably

Facing page: Crossbowman. A member of the vanguard of the infantry army in Pit No. 1. His crossbow could pierce shields and armour at 200 metres (656 feet).

Overleaf above: Chinese archaeologists at work on a corridor in the first pit. All the terracotta figures were damaged when the peasant army of Hsiang Yu devastated the Ch'in capital and the First Emperor's tomb.
Below: Charioteer and attendant officers from the first pit. Notice the scarves worn by these men in order to prevent the armour from rubbing their necks sore.

assisted by his minister Kuan Chung, turned Ch'i into the foremost state and the guardian of 'all that was good under Heaven'. The *pa* acted ostensibly on the behalf of the Chou king, but the protestations were rarely more than a cloak for his own policies. While Duke Huan preferred to resolve quarrels between states without recourse to war, a most laudable aim, the events of his own life reveal the actual uncertainties of the times. Duke Huan only gained the throne, which had been left vacant by the assassination of the preceding ruler in 686 BC, after a struggle with his own brother, whom he executed. On Duke Huan's own death in 643 BC his sons battled for the succession, delaying his funeral for two months. Worms were seen crawling out of the room in which the corpse reposed, and so putrid was the flesh that its dressing for burial could not be undertaken in daylight. Such a lack of deference was scandalous, a patent disregard of the ancestral cult.

From 685 till his own death in 645 BC, Kuan Chung provided Duke Huan with the kind of ministerial assistance King P'ing had yearned for. Pardoned by Duke Huan for being an ardent supporter of his rival brother – one of Kuan Chung's arrows fired during the conflict almost killed Duke Huan, striking the clasp of his belt – Kuan Chung more than repaid his master's clemency in guiding the state of Ch'i to an early supremacy. Economic provision was his first concern. Apart from the water-control scheme on the Yellow river, for drainage and irrigation purposes, and the development of salt-pans on the sea-coast, to raise state revenues on the production of salt, there is a possibility that Kuan Chung sponsored metallurgy. One historical text records Duke Huan as saying: 'The lovely metal is used for casting swords and pikes; it is used in company of dogs and horses. The ugly metal is used for casting hoes which flatten weeds and axes which fell trees; it is used upon the fruitful earth.'

Controversy has surrounded this reference to iron implements, bronze being 'the lovely metal' and iron 'the ugly'. Did the Iron Age start in China during the seventh century BC? Or was the Chan Kuo period its birthplace? Archaeological excavations so far suggest that iron appeared towards the very end of the Ch'un Ch'iu period. The adoption of iron implements was a revolutionary advance in agriculture, since the improved efficiency of ploughshares made cultivation easier. The increased productivity may account for the

Previous page above: Clearing the figures of armoured infantry in one of the corridors of Pit No. 1. Mr Yang Chen Ching, the curator of the site, is most concerned that the greatest care is taken in excavation and reconstruction.
Below: In the Ch'in armies only officers wore headgear. In the ranks a number of different hair styles probably indicate ethnic differences.

Facing page: This head has traces of pigment still visible. When the terracotta army was installed in the subterranean chambers all the soldiers and horses were brightly painted.

non-appearance of a large slave population in ancient China: a massive single labour force was not required to work the land, as in Roman Italy. But it was probably not until the Han dynasty, the successor to the Ch'in, that the manufacture of iron tools such as hoes, spades, sickles, axes, adzes, chisels and ploughshares reached a technical level sufficient to eclipse bronze. Chan Kuo iron implements are often found buried side by side with bronze and stone tools. Neither does the new metal seem to have had a profound impact on weapons of war until the Han period. Little iron has been unearthed from the warrior pits at Mount Li.

The increased farm production up to the reign of the First Emperor most probably resulted from the use of fertilizer and irrigation. The growth of towns and cities, based on the fortresses of nobles, may have been fostered by a labour surplus on the land: commerce and industry absorbed both food and people. The relative wealth of the city-dweller would have acted as a powerful magnet. We are told that an artisan or a merchant could earn five days' expenses by working one day, whereas a farmer could toil the year round and still not be able to feed himself.

The condition of the rural population was one of Kuan Chung's concerns. In the *Kuan Tzu*, a compilation of political observations associated with his name, there is an account of the harassed peasant, caught between the exactions of the tax-collector, who wanted his due before the time of harvest, and the mounting interest of the moneylender, who charged 100 per cent or more. The enlightened official was expected to come to his aid as poor harvests could not be sustained without tax relief. Ensuring the people's livelihood constituted one of the essential elements of government. The *Kuan Tzu* comments:

> *When the people are prosperous, they will be content with their rural communities and value their homes highly. Satisfied with their communities and valuing their homes will make them respect their superiors and be fearful of committing crimes. When they are respectful toward superiors and fearful of committing crimes, they are easy to govern. When people are poor, they create uneasy conditions in the countryside and show scant respect for their homes. When the countryside is uneasy and people are not concerned about their homes, they will dare to show disrespect to superiors and violate the laws.*

When they show disrespect to superiors and violate the laws, they are
difficult to govern. Thus it is that well-ordered states are always
prosperous while disorderly states always are poor. Therefore those
skilled in ruling will first enrich the people, and thereafter impose their
governing on them.

Though the *Kuan Tzu* was written down long after Kuan Chung's
ministry, it contains material directly relevant to Ch'un Ch'iu
statesmanship and remains a seminal work of Chinese political
thought. The elevation of the ruler's position anticipates Legalist
ideas, in particular those of Shang Yang (*c.* 390–338 BC) and Han Fei-
tzu (*c.* 280–233 BC), but without any disdain for the ordinary people.
The ruled were the resource from which the state was enriched and
strengthened, in effect the means to an end. They were not regarded
as being as stubborn and as stupid as beasts. Instead of the spurs and
whips of Legalist laws, the *Kuan Tzu* envisages a balance of
thoughtful policy and unthinking obedience, a firm and farsighted
ruler acting upon a deferential and diligent people. 'For the people
must obtain those things they want, and after that they will be
heedful of their superiors; after they have become heedful of their
superiors governing can be well carried out.'

The powers of the ruler were several. Sole arbiter of rewards and
punishments, a feudal lord like Duke Huan could grant life, kill,
enrich, impoverish, ennoble or debase. He took the lead in peace and
war, judiciously tempering 'majestic sternness' with 'gracious
kindness'. When he had to intimidate, he killed. When he wished to
encourage uprightness, he provided security. The moral character of
the ruler was not in question. The *Kuan Tzu* has Duke Huan admit to
avarice, drunkenness and lust. 'Bad things indeed,' Kuan Chung is
supposed to have replied, 'yet they are not crucial faults.' The
criterion of judgement can be none other than political success.

The glories of Duke Huan's hegemony were many. Confucius
told his disciples that the hegemon's campaigns against the northern
nomads had saved Chinese civilization. 'But for Kuan Chung,' he
said, 'we should now be wearing our garments buttoning on the side
and our hair down our backs.' He might have added the positive steps
that the Duke himself took to aid learning. Ch'i was the first state to
encourage scholars to take up residence in its capital, Lin-tzu. Other
immigrants included artisans and farmers, drawn from surrounding

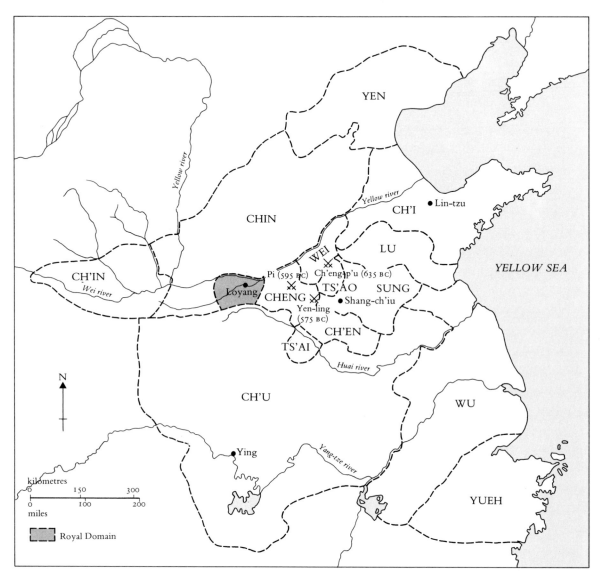

The major states of the Ch'un Ch'iu period (770–481 BC)

states by the better living conditions prevailing there. However, after Kuan Chung's death Duke Huan fell prey to household intriguers, notably a cook and a eunuch. The last two years of his reign undid the work of his famous minister and the ensuing family feud for the succession in 643 BC allowed the hegemony to pass first to Duke Siang of Sung, and then in 636 BC to Duke Wen of Chin. Less punctilious than previous hegemons, Duke Wen would summon the

92

Chou king to his conferences whenever he wanted him and dismiss the sovereign as soon as his presence was no longer required. This unceremonial treatment underlined the hollowness of the old feudal kingdom.

Only fourteen major states existed during the Ch'un Ch'iu period: Wei, on the lower reaches of the Yellow river; Ch'i, downstream and bordering the sea; Yen, the area around present-day Peking; Sung, in the middle Huai river valley; Ts'ao, a neighbour of Sung and annexed by that state in 487 BC; Lu, situated between Ch'i and Sung; Cheng, in the upper Huai river valley; Wu and Yueh, both on the lower reaches of the Yang-tze river; Ch'u, their western neighbour and conqueror in the Chan Kuo period; Ch'en and Ts'ai, other victims of Ch'u in the upper Huai river valley; Chin, the northern state which split subsequently into Chao, Han and a second Wei; and in the west Ch'in, the First Emperor's state. Their rivalry destroyed the tiny holdings along their borders, though joint action against aggression occasionally happened. For example, in 645 BC, when Ch'u invaded Hsu, a small territory adjacent to Cheng, the states of Lu, Ch'en, Wei, Cheng, Ts'ao, Ch'i and Hsu combined to resist the southern forces. But the frequency of armed conflict remained high throughout the Ch'un Ch'iu period, so that during his forty-two-year reign Duke Huan went to war no less than twenty-eight times.

The hegemon system did not keep the peace. The belligerence of the major states was matched by internal intrigue and violence, as powerful families within the aristocratic élite challenged the rulers themselves. In the growing confusion the practical approach of the *Kuan Tzu* had a strong appeal, especially as the balance of power swung in favour of two semi-barbarian states, Ch'in and Ch'u. If anything, the shift of the hegemony from Ch'i to Sung and Chin, then to Ch'in (629 BC) and Ch'u (613 BC), indicates that no single state possessed the power to dominate the Middle Kingdom, as China was now called.

The third hegemon, Duke Wen of Chin (ruled 635–628 BC), dealt a crushing blow to the ambitions of Ch'u at the battle of Ch'eng-p'u, when the army of the northern states routed that of Ch'u and its southern allies on the Wei-Ts'ao border in 632 BC. We are fortunate to know something of the action. In the winter of 633 BC Ch'u had besieged Shang-ch'iu, the capital of Sung, then an ally of Chin, and in the following spring Duke Wen led a large force to drive off the attackers. At the battle of Ch'eng-p'u Duke Wen outmanœuvred the Ch'u commander, the 'stubborn and uncouth' Tzu-yu, and scattered the southern contingents. Taking advantage of Tzu-yu's furious determination to slay him – the two men had been enemies ever since Wen as a youth had been taken hostage in Ch'u – Duke Wen lured the Ch'u left wing into a dangerous advance. Having immobilized the Ch'u right wing with an early thrust from the Chin left, the Chin right wing had pretended to fall back in disarray after taking a few casualties from arrows. Behind a screen of dust raised by chariots dragging trees, the Chin right wing and part of the Chin centre actually awaited the Ch'u charge which they smashed in a pincer movement of infantry and chariots, Tzu-yu falling among his exposed soldiers. Seeing the plight of both its wings, the Ch'u centre then turned and fled homewards.

Tactics were obviously important in the victory. The impetuous character of Tzu-yu also played a critical part. Yet the record in the *Tso-chuan* (*Tradition of Tso*), a work dating from between the late fourth and early second centuries BC, lays stress on ceremony and divination, the ritual before the commencement of fighting. We are told that Duke Wen undertook three withdrawals to fulfil a promise once given to the ruler of Ch'u, that he would retreat thrice rather than oppose his forces. Omens for the battle were zealously observed in hunting, dreams and songs, all as it happened favourable to Chin. Finally came the challenge, the promise to fight, the famous exchange between the Ch'u messenger and Duke Wen. 'Will Your Excellency permit our warriors and yours to play a game?' asked the messenger. 'Let me trouble you sir,' replied the duke, 'to tell your nobles to look to their chariots and honour their lord, for I shall see you at the crack of dawn.' Battle seems to have been regarded as the ultimate test of terrestrial authority, the moment when Heaven showed approval or disapproval of a lord's stewardship. It was divination writ large. In pious acknowledgement of Heaven's favour Duke Wen reported his victory to the Chou king at Loyang by sending to him 1,000 captured Ch'u soldiers and 100 chariots, each with four horses.

All was thought to occur within the sight of the ancestors. In time of war the expeditionary troops were given their orders in the ancestral temple; even the ancestral tablets were sometimes taken along when the ruler led the troops in person. At the battle of Yen-ling, fought near the Cheng-Sung border in 575 BC, the contestants made divinations 'before the spirits of the former rulers'. Seeking to avenge the defeat by Ch'u at nearby Pi twenty years earlier, the Duke of Chin entreated his illustrious ancestors to guide his spear in the engagement against Ch'u and Cheng. He asked that his sinews might not be injured, his bones not broken, and his face not wounded, so that success crowned his efforts and the ancestors avoided further disgrace. In the event Chin was victorious. But the three great battles, the triumphs of Chin at Ch'eng-p'u (632 BC) and Yen-ling (575 BC) and the triumph of Ch'u at Pi (595 BC), were all fought on the satellite territories of the two great powers, so that neither side was able to challenge effectively the other on home territory. Chin remained the leader of northern China and Ch'u continued to be the dominant power in the south.

Victors were expected to attend ancestral temples with prisoners. Captured men, equipment and supplies belonged to the ruler, who might distribute these spoils of war, as gifts for the deserving. In 594 BC a Chin general was rewarded with 1,000 families of defeated barbarians for having added new territory to the state. While Chin and Ch'in constantly sought to absorb the barbarian lands along their borders, the main era of expansion occurred during the Chan Kuo period. Prisoners of war, Chinese or barbarian, helped to change the nature of the Ch'un Ch'iu state. Enslaved well-born prisoners increased the wealth of lesser nobles, the families of ministers and officials becoming richer than the ruling houses in several states, and the prisoners who were left unransomed then lost status in enforced exile. Instances are recorded of envoys releasing fellow countrymen from the meanest occupations. In Chin a visiting minister of Ch'i encountered on the road a man carrying a bundle of hay on a piece of fur spread across his shoulders. Seeing the fur, the minister suspected the man was not really a peasant and upon inquiry discovered that he was a captive from his own state. Immediately the minister unhitched one of his chariot horses and used it to buy the freedom of his fellow countryman.

Not all of the vanquished nobles were treated like this Ch'i prisoner. In 538 BC the duke of Ch'u spared the ruling house of Lai, a small state in the Huai river valley. Defeated rulers were usually deposed and occasionally put to death as sacrificial victims. There was a ritual of surrender in which a vanquished lord presented himself and his own coffin to the victor. Nevertheless, in the Ch'un Ch'iu period slaughter seems rarely to have been indiscriminate. The histories speak of 'blood for the drums', possibly the ceremonial execution of certain prisoners after the battle; the formula may also refer to the blood of the slain, whether killed in battle or executed afterwards. Where the *Tso-chuan* definitely records human sacrifice, the slaying of the prisoners is roundly condemned.

Warfare for the Ch'un Ch'iu nobleman contained what in Europe would be termed chivalry. There were accepted procedures for joining battle as well as determining whether or not to fight at all. Once the divination was over and the decision had been taken to give battle, brave nobles from either side would mount daring raids in order to provoke or intimidate their opponents. They engaged in archery duels from speeding chariots, often taking immense personal risks. Before the battle of Pi three Ch'u heroes skirmished the Chin lines: one drove the chariot, the second loosed arrows, and the third acted as spearman. Pursued by a squadron of Chin charioteers, the Ch'u adventurers were making a daring escape, when a stag leaped up before them and they downed it with their last arrow. As a consequence of this, they halted and presented the beast to their pursuers, who accepted the gift and broke off the chase. In letting the Ch'u chariot get away the Chin nobles had acknowledged the prowess and politeness of their foe. Another instance of courtesy which took place after the battle of Pi is wonderfully ironic. A retreating Chin chariot got stuck in a rut and when a Ch'u soldier advised him on how to overcome the difficulty, the annoyed Chin charioteer remarked, 'We cannot equal your great state in the number of times we have run away!' The charisma of the nobility derived in part from the court around the ancestral temple, the ceremonial directly beneath the gaze of the deified dead; partly, it was kept alive in the minds of the people through the mannered glories of the battlefield. It was only the abandonment of the chariot in favour of the deadly shafts of the crossbow during the fourth century BC that weakened the link between the aristocracy and war. The ultimate downgrading of the status of the military in Chinese society was a later achievement of Confucianism, especially under the Han emperors.

The hegemony of Chin, the biggest of the northern states, was challenged by Ch'in, a western neighbour, and Ch'u, the biggest southern state. These two semi-barbaric lands dominated the later Chan Kuo period; indeed the drive towards imperial unification might be said to have been a race between Ch'in and Ch'u.

Originally Ch'in was a small fief on the upper reaches of the Wei river, to the west of the old royal domain of Chou. After the disaster of 771 BC and the removal of the capital from Hao to Loyang, the defence of the western frontier was left to the lord of Ch'in, who in recompense for such a dangerous service received most of the abandoned royal domain. According to one tradition, the house of Ch'in descended from a horsedealer, probably implying non-Chinese stock. Up until 266 BC a noble of Wei could remark that 'Ch'in has the same customs as the Jung and Ti tribes. It has the heart of a tiger or a wolf. It is greedy and untrustworthy. It is ignorant of polite manners, proper relationships, and upright behaviour. Whenever the opportunity for gain arises, it will treat relatives as if they were mere animals.' Although the cultural backwardness of Ch'in was a byword even at the end of the Chan Kuo period, no state had gained more from the help of alien residents. The leading statesmen of Ch'in came from the more civilized states. They were attracted by the reluctance of Ch'in rulers to be circumscribed by feudalism. This lack of enthusiasm for courtly etiquette cannot simply be attributed to barbarian origins. The Chou dynasts themselves seem to have led a semi-barbarian, semi-civilized people against the Shang. Whereas the Chou kingdom was characterized by ceremonial, albeit a sham during the stay at Loyang, the state of Ch'in eschewed aristocratic pretensions and embraced mundane tasks, such as the improvement of agriculture and metallurgy. The timing of the augmentation of territory may have a bearing on its more down-to-earth character. The house of Ch'in inherited the domain of a disgraced ruler as well as the pressing need to master the barbarian intruders. Building up its own power base was a necessity, a condition of survival. There was neither room nor time for anything else. The state of Ch'in always had to rely on itself.

Independence and innovation mark the progress of Ch'in down to the reign of the First Emperor. No doubt the initial adjustment of the dukes of Ch'in to their role as defenders of the western march influenced this development, especially if they came to an agreement with barbarian neighbours by incorporating tractable peoples and tolerating their customs, but the resilience and strength of the state really derived from effective management inside a natural stronghold, the Land within the Passes. Once the means of withstanding barbarian pressures from the north and west had been devised, Ch'in was free to advance on its feudal neighbours to the east and south, or to seal the passes into the Wei river valley against expeditionary forces approaching from those directions. Ch'in established a military reputation quickly. While it was treated by the other states as something apart from the rest of the Middle Kingdom, the excellence of Ch'in soldiers on the battlefield was understood. Opposing armies knew they would be swiftly and fiercely attacked.

In the last century of the Ch'un Ch'iu period Ch'in was involved in a triangular struggle with Chin and Ch'u, the eastern state of Ch'i having been gravely weakened through internal conflict. Sometimes Ch'u and Ch'in struck at Chin. Sometimes Ch'in resisted both Chin and Ch'u. The equilibrium was not upset till 453 BC, when clan warfare did even worse for Chin than it had done for Ch'i. By 403 BC Chin had disintegrated, leaving Ch'in in a strong position along the Yellow river valley.

For Ch'u the best years occurred in the hegemony of Duke Chuang (613–591 BC). His skill as a general and statesman compelled the Middle Kingdom to recognize this sprawling, mysterious land as an organized state. Ch'u aggression against the northern nomads in 606 BC was welcomed, though the hegemon's attitude towards the Loyang caused alarm. Duke Chuang daringly inquired about the size and weight of the Nine Tripods, since time immemorial the symbol of kingship. Was not this an example of barbarian arrogance? As with Ch'in, the reaction of the older feudal states needs to be viewed with caution. The Yang-tze was a long way from the Yellow river; its inhabitants comprised a number of distinct peoples; the watery enviroment had little in common with the northern mountains and plains; yet, the sinicization of the region was well advanced in the Ch'un Ch'iu period. Ch'u's absorption of so many feudal territories had at least seen to that. The dukes of Ch'u also pacified the lands bordering on the south-east coast, in the process facilitating the evolution of Wu, a state in the Yang-tze delta region, and Yueh, another state in the mountains to the south. Of the two, Yueh was definitely peripheral to Chou culture, its people being entirely non-Chinese. Nevertheless, the feudal order in Ch'u had relatively shallow foundations, and in consequence it was already disposed towards Legalist doctrines on princely authority. Penal law was well established in the Ch'un Ch'iu period. A disagreement which Confucius had with an elder statesman of Ch'u illustrates this. Whereas the Ch'u noble saw loyalty to the state as an individual's first duty, the philosopher maintained it was loyalty to the family. 'Among us,' said the Ch'u lord, 'there are those who are so upright that if his father steals a sheep, the son will testify against him.' Confucius replied, 'Among us the upright act quite differently. The son shields the father, and the father shields the son; we regard this as uprightness.' The Legalist tendency of Ch'u may have sprung from a looser kinship system, but the relative unimportance of clan ties should not lead us to suppose that the state was spared the family feuds which troubled its neighbours. On the contrary, the might of Ch'u was contained through the activities of exiles abroad, and in Wu above all.

The defection of Wu Ch'en in 584 BC cost Ch'u its security in the east. This maligned general taught the soldiers of Wu how to use weapons and fight in formation. An equally distinguished citizen of Ch'u named Wu Tzu-hsu was obliged to seek refuge in Wu over half a century later. Wu Tzu-hsu fled the unjust wrath of the Ch'u ruler, who had killed his father and brother. Vengeance was his sole aim, Ssu-ma Ch'ien tells us in his *Shih Chi* (*Historical Records*). It shaped the refugee's life as well as the lives of people caught up in the war he engineered between Wu and Ch'u. As the duke of Wu's adviser, Wu Tzu-hsu mobilized the strength of the new state against the hated house of Ch'u. In 506 BC the fall of Ying, the Ch'u capital, shocked the Middle Kingdom. Five times the Wu army routed the superior forces of Ch'u, who were unable to drive back the water-borne invaders unaided. Only the arrival of troops sent by incredulous Ch'in halted the advance and after seven battles forced a Wu evacuation. 'At this time Wu,' the *Shih Chi* tersely notes, 'employing strategies Wu Tzu-hsu suggested, crushed the powerful state of Ch'u in the west, filled Ch'i and Chin to the north of it with awe, and in the south forced the people of Yueh to submit.'

This significant military presence on its eastern border limited the role Ch'u wished to play in the north. Relief appeared to have come in 473 BC when Yueh overran Wu, the latter's main army being then committed to a northern expedition against Lu and Ch'i. However, Ch'u sighed in vain because for the next seventy-four years Yueh controlled the lower Yang-tze valley. Not until 333 BC could a revitalized Ch'u win a conclusive victory over Yueh and absorb the majority of its territory. It is interesting to note that Wu and Yueh rose to eminence with infantry armies. Because the lands of the Yang-tze delta and the mountainous south-east coast did not lend themselves to charioteering, new methods of fighting were evolved there. Another innovation by Wu was the use of ships, both at sea and on rivers. The Wu army penetrated Ch'u along the course of the Yang-tze river (506 BC) and a fleet raided northwards as far as Ch'i (486 BC). These military developments anticipated the large-scale wars of the Chan Kuo states, for which planning and preparation seem to have exhausted the best energies of the contenders.

The difficulties confronting Ch'u in the Yang-tze valley ended the hegemon system. After the hegemony of Duke Chuang of Ch'u the *pa* institution faded away. No state had the capacity to coerce its rivals. Ch'in concentrated on its own development, Ch'i and Chin were racked by internal disorder, and Ch'u battled with Wu, then Yueh. In the final run-down of feudalism there was a widespread adoption of the title *wang*, or king: no longer was the Chou ruler of Loyang the supreme monarch of China, every and any ruler styled himself as king. The balance of power disappeared completely at the close of the Ch'u Ch'iu period. In 546 BC the chief minister of Sung, one of the smaller central states that had suffered terribly in the struggle between Chin and Ch'u, took the initiative in calling a peace conference at Shang-ch'iu. The agreement lasted for a generation, when it was breached by Wu, a non-signatory. The Chan Kuo period came about as a result of this resumption of hostilities. These years were to witness the death throes of feudal society and end in the unification of all China – the foundation of the first Chinese empire under Ch'in.

Chapter Four

The Triumph of Ch'in; the Chan Kuo period, 481-221 BC

In 403 BC internal trouble split Chin into three separate states: Han, Wei and Chao. This disintegration removed from the Yellow river valley the only serious rival of Ch'in. Taking advantage of the opportunity, successive kings developed the power base until Ch'in could match and defeat Ch'u, the southern contender for supremacy. Powerless, the Chou monarch, the Son of Heaven, could only watch as these two great powers, still incompletely sinicized, gained territory through the quarrels of the other feudal states. Intensification of war between the Seven States – Ch'i, Yen, Chao, Han, Wei, Ch'in and Ch'u – marked the Chan Kuo or Warring States period, named after a collection of historical anecdotes, the *Chan-kuo Ts'e (Intrigues of the Warring States)*. No longer were interstate issues settled by conferences or diplomacy: to the battlefield went all matters of dispute. Everywhere the lack of harmonious relationships afflicted daily life. With the feudal princes bent on increasing their power, the ministers in the feudal states soon followed suit, and disorder spread from rank to rank. Instability was normal. China experienced a series of profound social changes as the old order of the Ch'un Ch'iu period disappeared and a new order emerged.

Typical of the political and social ferment going on at the outset of the Chan Kuo period was the once famous state of Ch'i. For a while it appeared to be about to disintegrate, like Chin. The collapse of Ch'i was forestalled in 391 BC, when a ministerial family seized power, exiled the ruler, and reorganized the state with its own supporters. The usurping family were the Ch'en, who had settled in Ch'i under the first hegemon, Duke Huan. That this family could appropriate the throne of such a respected state and receive the nominal recognition of Loyang – a blatant disregard of the hereditary

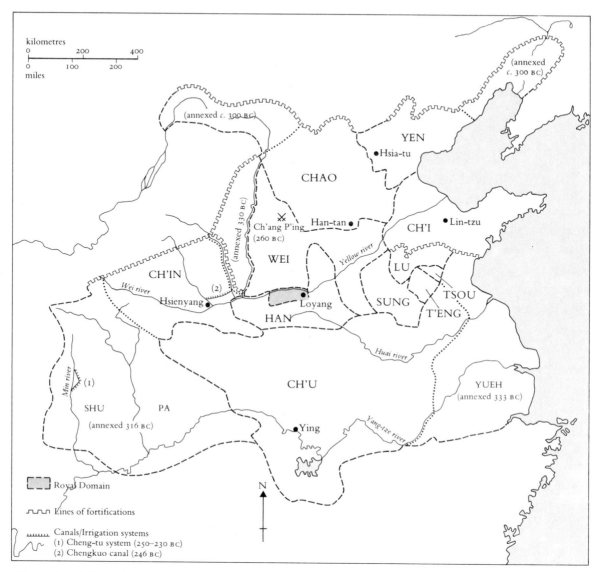

Chan Kuo China (481–221 BC)   *The Seven States, the major contenders for supremacy, were Ch'i, Yen, Chao, Han, Wei, Ch'in and Ch'u.*

principle – shows how far times had changed. The Ch'en had been steadily acquiring influence for generations by seeking the goodwill of the population. They were generous with aid during famine and their moneylenders conducted business in an ungrasping manner, whereas the state government taxed heavily and imposed a harsh penal law. In the internal crisis the people not surprisingly turned to the Ch'en.

Other states possessed the equivalent of the Ch'en; in neighbouring Sung, for example, one ruler gained the throne by being generous to the people when the crops failed. None of these usurpers came from Ch'un Ch'iu ministerial families, who during the Chan Kuo era do not in fact appear in the historical records. The newly powerful were *shih*, the educated sons of the lesser nobility and the most able and talented commoners. The *shih* ran the feudal administration and held non-hereditable offices, including that of magistrate of an area that had formerly been the fief of a minister. Increasingly, towards the close of the Ch'un Ch'iu period magistrates had rebelled against their feudal masters.

The changing nature of warfare in the Chan Kuo period continued the process of downgrading the aristocracy. Changes in military technique made the chariot-riding nobleman an anachronism. As war became more intense and deadly, the Seven States were obliged to rely on infantry armies, better equipped and organized forces than had ever taken the field in Ch'un Ch'iu times. Conscription of commoners placed war on a grand scale, as armies numbering hundreds of thousands crashed into each other. Even the small state of Han could maintain a striking force of 300,000 men, while Ch'in and Ch'u were able to support armies of more than 1,000,000 men. In these changed circumstances noble birth was no advantage, and noble upbringing may have been a handicap on the battlefield.

The chariot, however, had never been a really efficient fighting machine. As early as 541 BC a Chin general had abandoned chariots and reorganized his soldiers into infantry squads in order to deal with barbarians along the mountainous northern frontier. The king of Chao, who inherited the same military problem during the Chan Kuo period, in 307 BC went so far as to adopt the barbarian fashion of wearing trousers, for his newly formed light cavalry. This imitation of nomad horse tactics proved useful on the borders of the steppe, where high speed was needed to counter sudden raids, but it did little to influence either the armoured masses of infantry or those lethal auxiliaries, the crossbowmen, whose weapon was the most dominant during battles of the Chan Kuo period.

Dismembered Chin was not untraditional merely in warfare. Han, Chao and Wei underwent a political reformation that removed the last vestiges of feudalism. Instrumental in this reform was Sheng Pu-hai (*c.* 400–337 BC), a man of humble origin who served as chief counsellor of Han for seventeen years. After studying government and administration, he convinced the Han ruler of his ability to run the state. Sheng Pu-hai's writings exist only in fragments but indicate a concern for efficient administration; indeed, his discussion of methods or techniques (*shu*) point towards a bureaucratic state. The later philosopher Han Fei-tzu summarized Sheng Pu-hai's theory of government as appointing officials according to ability, demanding that they perform the duties of office, examining the worth of all ministers, and keeping control of justice. Although Sheng Pu-hai stressed the role of the ruler, he advocated the use of neither naked power nor harsh punishments unlike the full-blooded Legalist Shang Yang, his contemporary and adviser to rival Ch'in. In Han the ruler was expected to govern firmly and hold his officials responsible for their actions. Yet strictness in the application of penalties in the state of Han remained chilling. When on one occasion Sheng Pu-hai's lord got drunk and fell asleep in a cold place, the crown-keeper put a coat over him. Coming to, the ruler asked who had covered him, and being informed, punished the coat-keeper but put the crown-keeper to death, on the principle that stepping outside the duties of an office was worse than negligence.

Han Fei-tzu, who quoted this judgment with approval, pointed out that 'Shen Pu-hai advocated methods and Shang Yang advocated law'; but experienced though these statesmen were in 'great matters', still 'with respect to law and methods, the two both failed to achieve perfection'. According to Han Fei-tzu a combination of strict supervision and pitiless punishment was required for the security of a state. It was a view that appealed to the future First Emperor, when a dozen or so years before unification he wecomed Han Fei-tzu to Ch'in. The visit ended with the death of the philosopher, a victim of Li Ssu's enmity.

Ch'in, Chao, Wei, Han and Ch'u were states disposed towards new methods of organization. However, it is curious that, although Ch'in made such use of the reforming Legalists, not one of the Legalists was born in Ch'in. Li Ssu was a native of Ch'u and Kung-sun Yang, or Shang Yang, came from Wei. Because learning hardly existed in Ch'in, its rulers were forced to look beyond their boundaries for people to employ. The career of the alien Shang Yang there from 350 to 338 BC brought about far-reaching changes. Under his administration the nobles were suppressed, a new social order based on military merit was created, and officials ruled the people in the interests of the state, without regard to familial or religious traditions. In hastening the tendency of the age – increased authoritarianism of the state and despotism of the ruler – Shang Yang made the Ch'in government the most powerful, and the Ch'in people the most disciplined, in the Middle Kingdom.

At the beginning of the *Shang-chun shu (Book of Lord Shang)* occurs an argument between the would-be reformer and the conservatives before the Ch'in ruler. It concerns the sanctity of customary law. Whereas the conservative Ch'in counsellors urged King Hsiao to follow established practice in all things, Shang Yang recommended a complete break with past customs. 'A wise man,' he said, 'creates laws, but a worthless man is controlled by them; a man of talent reforms rites, but a worthless man is enslaved by them. With a man who is controlled by laws, it is useless to discuss change; with a man who is enslaved by rites, it is useless to discuss reform. Let your Highness not hesitate.' Persuaded at last by Shang Yang's approach to government, King Hsiao concluded: 'One should in one's plans be directed by the needs of the moment – I have no doubt about it.' The trust of the king in his reforming minister was well repaid. Shang Yang's dedication, his subservience to the throne's wishes, bordered on the fanatical. When the crown prince transgressed one of the new laws, Shang Yang demanded that he be punished like everyone else. The widespread complaints over his measures and edicts compelled the reformer to stand firm on the issue, though he knew that the heir apparent could not be harmed. Therefore, King Hsaio agreed that the prince's guardian should be degraded and that the face of the prince's tutor be tattoed, presumably on the grounds that these unfortunate nobles were held responsible for the prince's misbehaviour. It is said that from the following day onwards all the people in Ch'in obeyed the laws. Yet this fanaticism brought Shang Yang to his own undoing. Unloved, and feared by the nobility and the common people alike, he was safe only as long as King Hsiao reigned. After the accession of the crown prince in 338 BC, Shang Yang's enemies swiftly accused him of sedition and officers were sent to arrest him. The fleeing minister at first sought refuge in an obscure inn but the inn-keeper, ignorant of his identity, informed him that under the laws of Lord Shang he dared not admit a man without a permit for fear of punishment. Equally fruitless was Shang Yang's flight to the state of Wei, where his past aggression still rankled and fear of the power of newly reformed Ch'in prevailed. There was no escape. Returning to his estates in Ch'in, Shang Yang raised local troops and opposed the royal army sent against him. Defeat, death and dismemberment were his fate. As an example to the rebellious, the corpse of Shang Yang was torn limb from limb by chariots. His family was also exterminated.

The Confucianist Ssu-ma Ch'ien felt that 'the bad end Shang Yang finally came to in Ch'in was no more than he deserved'. At the close of his biography in the *Shih Chi*, Ssu-ma Ch'ien lists the Legalist reformer's faults as dishonesty, guile and inhumanity. He adds that they are also to be found in his writings. As an honest historian though, Ssu-ma Ch'ien does record the achievement of Shang Yang's ministry.

> *By the end of ten years the Ch'in people were acquiescent. Nothing lost on the road was picked up and pocketed, the hills were free of bandits, every household prospered, men fought bravely on the battlefield but avoided quarrels at home, and good government existed in both towns and villages.*

Shang Yang had imposed law (*fa*) on Ch'in. The state ran smoothly and quietly. When some of the conservative critics of his policies began to praise their results, Shang Yang branded them as trouble-makers and banished them to frontier settlements. 'In an orderly country,' the *Book of Lord Shang* asserts, 'punishments are numerous and rewards are rare.' To Shang Yang the key activities of the state were agriculture and war: he declared that the ruler should beware lest individuals 'occupy themselves with trade and practise arts and crafts, all in order to avoid agriculture and war. . . . Where the people are given to such pursuits, it is certain that such a country will be dismembered.' It was essential to husband agricultural output, ensuring that all available land was sown and that all surplus grain was stored, in order to feed the enormous armies, perhaps ten times larger than those of the Ch'un Ch'iu period. The Legalist philosophers would have liked virtually to destroy all thought, learning and culture, and to fashion government and society into a fighting machine.

Although orderliness and strength were also the aims of Chao, Wei, Han and Ch'u, in none of these states were such policies as successful as Shang Yang's in Ch'in. The degree of centralization he established was unique. In perspective it can be seen that his ministry was a watershed, a point in time from which flowed the course of events leading to the defeudalization of China under the First Emperor. Shang Yang's laws made possible the bureaucratic administration instituted by Li Ssu, Ch'in Shih-huang-ti's Grand Councillor.

Shang Yang's reforms had an economic as well as a political thrust. His most crucial change of law was the abolition of the system under which peasant farmers were attached to the land of their overlords. Henceforth a free peasantry could itself own land. Without doubt this new freedom encouraged immigration to thinly populated Ch'in as did later incentives such as houses and exemption from military service. Shang Yang stimulated internal migration to uncultivated areas through measures directed against the family. Persons who had two or more adult sons living with them were required to pay a double tax. Another law prohibited fathers, sons and brothers from living in the same room. The rich were discouraged from staying together by the extra tax: the poor found their dwellings too small for all their close relations to have separate rooms. Under the new law some members of the family had to move out of the household and earn a separate living. This reduction in the size of the family also curbed clan influence, as the greater emphasis on individualism undermined the authority of the head of the household, who lost control of family members and family possessions. In a memorandum to the throne, the Han statesman Chia I (201–169 BC) deplored the loss of civility involved, warning the emperor that such enactments destroyed the attitude of subordination and politeness advocated by Confucius. He wrote in 174 BC that

Lord Shang abandoned propriety, discarded benevolence, and concentrated his attention on the development of the state. After his laws had been in operation for two years, the customs of Ch'in disappeared daily. So it happened that a rich man had to send away his son with a

*share of the family property when he reached adulthood, and a poor man
had to make his son another's servant. So bad did things become that a
son who lent a rake or hoe to his father appeared a veritable benefactor,
and a mother who took a daughter's dustpan or broom might be called a
thief by her own kin.*

The ideal of the Confucianists found no space in Shang Yang's Ch'in.
Yet what we recognize today as the traditional Chinese family, the
cornerstone of Chinese civilization right into the modern era, only
evolved after the Ch'in empire. Confucian philosophers in the Chan
Kuo period were largely peripheral to society. Furthermore, the
teachings of Confucius would have made little headway in unsophisticated Ch'in. Even in Chia I's lifetime the Ch'in people were
still considered less civilized. Shang Yang's laws obviously had an
impact on family structure and social attitudes, but it is impossible to
tell how far he legalized a practice already in existence. Both land
transfer and individualist behaviour were probably common before
Shang Yang's ministry.

Shang Yang made collective responsibility more important than
the family as a method of control. The people were organized into
groups of fives or tens mutually responsible for each other. They
were obliged to report one another's crimes and, if they failed to do
this they were obliged to share one another's punishments when the
crime was discovered. The relatives of the five or ten men concerned
were held to be equally guilty. A law of 746 BC had provided for the
execution of the three *tsu*, kindred to the third degree, for certain
crimes, and Shang Yang applied this rigorously. It was a fundamental
tenet of his philosophy that the severity of the law deterred crime. To
litter the streets of Hsienyang, the Ch'in capital, was deemed worthy
of flogging, and law officers had a repertoire of terrible punishments:
besides death, there was bodily mutilation, such as cutting off the
nose, branding on top of the head, tattooing the face, extracting ribs,
and boiling in a cauldron. Imposition of Ch'in law on a united China
under the First Emperor toppled the remaining pillars of feudalism.
In the end rebellion against these over-harsh laws also toppled the
Ch'in dynasty itself.

We need, however, to exercise caution in our view of Ch'in, not
least because its history was written up by its Confucian successor.

Chia I's memorial doubtless contains a fairly accurate description of Ch'in social life, but it would be wrong to assume that all of Shang Yang's measures continued unchanged after 338 BC. The reformer's distaste for philosophical discussion was not shared by Lu Pu-wei, chief adviser to King Chuang-hsiang and to the future First Emperor until his fall in 237 BC. Lu Pu-wei invited scholars to Hsienyang and ordered their thoughts to be recorded in a book more than 200,000 words long. The repression of learning under the First Emperor was a return to a stricter Legalist approach, though the real burning of the books occurred in 206 BC, when a rebel army fired Hsienyang and destroyed the imperial library.

One policy decision of Shang Yang that was maintained relates to the administration of the state. In 350 BC he reorganized Ch'in into thirty-one *hsien*, districts administered by an official appointed by and responsible to the king. Except for the small estates possessed by the Ch'in royal family and senior ministers, land was thereupon dissociated from nobility. A new aristocratic hierarchy of eighteen ranks, with purely honorary titles, replaced the old territorial and hereditary system. Ennoblement could only be achieved by valour until about 250 BC, when both military exploits and money became acceptable. Though the *hsien* was not exclusive to Ch'in – it was used in other states as a means of dealing with newly conquered territory or the lands of dispossessed rebels – Shang Yang employed administrative districts in a more effective and systematic way than anyone else. Under Ch'in Shih-huang-ti this institution of central control was to be extended to the whole of China.

Since 316 BC the lands of Shu and Pa, approximately modern Szechuan, had acknowledged Ch'in suzerainty, much to the annoyance of outflanked Ch'u. However, in 285 BC the land of Shu threatened revolt and was converted from a dependent territory into a *chun*, or commandery. The strategic and economic value of Shu obliged Ch'in to incorporate the whole region into its administrative organization and in consequence the commandery was subdivided into a number of *hsien*. Today the prosperity of Szechuan still rests on the water-conservancy scheme introduced by Li Ping (died *c.* 240 BC), an early Ch'in governor. Through his initiative in about 250 BC, Shu was transformed into a valuable asset. He persuaded both the non-Chinese inhabitants and the new colonists to undertake the construction of a remarkable system of irrigation; the central work of the scheme was a dam which divided the Min river into two streams. While one of the streams acted as a flood channel and carried boat traffic, the other branched out into numerous small canals feeding an intricate network of thousands of irrigation ditches. People soon called the plain 'sea-on-land'. The soundness of Li Ping's engineering seems to indicate that the basic principles of hydraulics must have been known in the third century BC. The errors of Duke Huan of Ch'i were apparently avoided. A poetical comment put up in a commemorative temple at the site of the dam encapsulates Li Ping's theory. The poet remarks

'*Dig the channel deep*
And keep the dikes low.'
This Six-Character Teaching
Holds good for a thousand autumns.

In the *Shih Chi* the Min river scheme is mentioned in a single sentence. This does not mean that Ssu-ma Ch'ien undervalued irrigation and canal-building. Quite the contrary, he was the first Chinese historian to appreciate the fundamental importance of the increase in productivity and the supply potential for the ultimate political success of Ch'in. What gripped his attention was the intrigue behind the construction of Ch'in's other great water-conservancy scheme, the Chengkuo canal. Ssu-ma Ch'ien records:

That the king of Han wished to prevent the eastern expansion of Ch'in by exhausting it with projects. He therefore sent the water engineer, Cheng Kuo, to the king of Ch'in to convince him that a canal should be built between the Ching and the Lo rivers. The proposed canal would be 300 li long and used for irrigation. The project was half finished when the trick was discovered. The Ch'in ruler was stopped from killing Cheng Kuo by the engineer's own argument. 'Although this scheme was intended to injure you,' he said, 'if the canal is completed, it will bring great benefit to your state.' The work was then ordered to be continued. When finished it irrigated 40,000 ch'ing of poor land with water laden with rich silt. The productivity of the fields rose to one chung *for each* mu. *Thus, the interior became a fertile plain without bad years. Ch'in, then, grew rich and strong and finally conquered all other feudal states. The canal was called after Cheng Kuo, who built it.*

The plot misfired badly; Han had bestowed on Ch'in the means of eventual victory. The additional grain from this vast area, about 227,000 hectares (560,929 acres), supported extra soldiers and the strategic advantage of the canal (124 kilometres (77 miles) in length) was greatly improved communications. The Chengkuo canal, opened in the year 246 BC, transformed the Land within the Passes into the first key economic area, a place where agricultural productivity and facilities for transport permitted a supply of tax-grain so superior to that of other places, that the ruler who controlled it could control all China.

It is interesting that the Han king assumed the willingness of Ch'in to adopt public works on a scale greater that any other state. The legacy of Shang Yang's ministry must have been the linking of Ch'in with innovation. The project was so extensive that even the Ch'in ruler hesitated on hearing of the plot, though he was persuaded to continue by the engineer, who may have only realized himself during the course of the work what it would mean for Ch'in once it had been completed. Another account of the interview has Cheng Kuo saying: 'I have, by this ruse, prolonged the life of the state of Han for a few years, but I am accomplishing a scheme which will sustain the state of Ch'in for ten thousand generations.' Though history was to deny the Ch'in dynasty such ascendancy, Cheng Kuo's estimation of the long-term affect on the balance of power in China was not inaccurate. The last dynasty to have its capital in the Wei river valley was the T'ang (AD 618–906).

The construction of large-scale irrigation schemes became a settled policy on the part of Ch'in rulers, as they contributed directly to the Legalist goals of agriculture and war. Other works commissioned by the throne included the buildings of walls and bridges. Shortly after 300 BC a long wall was built to resist pressure from the northern nomads. Its building constituted one of the first steps in the making of the famous Great Wall, which was later completed under Ch'in Shih-huang-ti. The growing interest of Ch'in in the lower Yellow river valley is evident in the placing of one bridge across the Wei river and another across the Yellow river itself. The Wei bridge near Hsienyang, in use by 290 BC, comprised sixty-eight spans of about nine metres (thirty feet) each, giving an overall measurement of more than 600 metres (1,970 feet). While all its beams were of wood,

carrying a deck width of twelve metres (forty feet), some of the
piers close to the city were of stone. The Yellow river bridge
was entirely composed of boats, a method inherited from the Chou
people. The great floating bridge, sited in 257 BC hard by the junc-
tion of the Wei and Yellow rivers, lasted for many centuries.
Organizing such public enterprises greatly increased the central
authority of the king, whose officials were responsible for every
detail of planning, building and upkeep. It was through their
activities that a more streamlined state emerged, the predecessor
of the bureaucratic system of the Chinese empire.

In Ch'in the court had ceased to be the preserve of the high-born.
Lu Pu-wei, originally a merchant in Han-tan, the Chao capital, was a
successful and respected minister. In that city he met Prince Tzu-chu
of Ch'in who was being kept as a hostage and suffered discomfort
there through inadequate funds. According to Ssu-ma Ch'ien, Lu
Pu-wei seized the opportunity of assisting the prince for his own
ends. 'Here is some rare merchandise that may be stored up', he is
reputed to have remarked. Using his wealth the merchant caused the
almost forgotten prince to be named heir apparent to the Ch'in
throne. While Prince Tzu-chu received gold enough to live in style
and impress his feudal peers at the Chao court, Lu Pu-wei travelled to
the Ch'in court loaded with fine presents for Tzu-chu's relations.
Having gained the ear of the favourite wife of the Prince An-kuo, the
crown prince, he induced this childless lady to adopt Tzu-chu as her
son. Lu Pu-wei advised her thus:

> When a woman serves a man with her beauty, I have heard that as her
> beauty fades, his love slackens too. Now Your Ladyship serves the
> Crown Prince, who deeply loves you, though you are without children.
> Why do you not now attach to yourself one of the royal princes who is
> worthy and filial, establish him as the successor, and make him your
> son? During your lifetime you will be deeply honoured and afterwards
> your son as king will preserve your memory.

So it was that Tzu-chu was declared the son of Prince An-kuo and Li
Pu-wei was appointed as his guardian. When in 251 BC Prince An-
kuo acceded to the throne as King Hsiao-wen, Prince Tzu-chu and
his guardian were summoned to the Ch'in court. The sudden death
of King Hsiao-wen in the ensuing year meant that Lu Pu-wei's

protégé was crowned as King Chuang-hsiang. The investor's reward was greater than anything he might have obtained from commerce: he was made Grand Councillor, addressed as 'Uncle' by the Ch'in ruler, and allowed the revenues of 100,000 households. If the authority of Lu Pu-wei was considerable during the short reign of Chuang-hsiang (250–247 BC), it was virtually absolute for the minority of the king's young son, Prince Cheng, the future First Emperor. For a decade the ex-merchant was the power in Hsienyang, where he maintained 3,000 visiting scholars, one of whom was Li Ssu. Then in 237 BC Lu Pu-wei was involved in a scandal concerning the queen mother and dismissed from office. Banished to remote Shu, he committed suicide by drinking poison two years later.

The career of Lu Pu-wei was unique. There is no other known instance of financial backing for a prince coming from a merchant. While Ch'in was acknowledged to be in many respects unlike the rest of the Middle Kingdom, the 'selling' of a king remains a singular event. It indicates a great change from the Ch'un Ch'iu era when merchants were little better than dependants of noble households.

The unusualness of Lu Pu-wei's premiership may also account for the idea that he, and not King Chuang-hsiang, was the father of Prince Cheng. The *Shih Chi* tells us that

> *Among the courtesans of Han-tan, Lu Pu-wei enjoyed one who was a beauty and a dancer. He kept her and knew she was pregnant. When Prince Tzu-chu was once drinking in Lu Pu-wei's house, he saw and liked her, and asked if he might have her. Though annoyed, Lu Pu-wei decided that he was too far committed to the prince to refuse the request, and thought that in obliging him he might hook something rare. So he gave up his concubine, who kept to herself the secret of her pregnancy. When in time she bore a son, Cheng, the prince established her as his proper wife.*

The same lady in 237 BC caused Lu Pu-wei's downfall. Ssu-ma Ch'ien in his biography of the merchant blames everything on the lasciviousness of the First Emperor's mother. According to the *Shih Chi*, while Ch'in Shih-huang-ti was still a minor, Lu Pu-wei and the queen mother had secret sexual relations. Fearing that the young king would find out one day about this illicit affair, Lu Pu-wei looked for another man to take his place. He chose a certain Lao Ai, who possessed a tremendous phallus. So impressed was the queen mother with her new lover that she not only gave birth secretly to two children but also allowed Lao Ai to plot for their succession. News of this disorderly conduct reached the ears of King Cheng in 238 BC and he sent an official to investigate the matter. As a result Lao Ai and his kindred were exterminated to the third degree, Lu Pu-wei was debased, and the queen mother lost her liberty of movement. 'The king wished to kill the Grand Councillor, but because he had done much for the preceding ruler, and because his retainers and scholarly supporters . . . were numerous, the king did not allow the law to be applied.'

These are the circumstances of Lu Pu-wei's fall as they appear in the biography left by Ssu-ma Ch'ien. The story of the First Emperor's illegitimacy and the wantonness of his mother is probably an interpolation. Elsewhere in the *Shih Chi* we read that 'the First Emperor was the son of King Chuang-hsiang of Ch'in. While King Chuang-hsiang as a prince was a hostage in Chao, he saw the concubine of Lu Pu-wei. He liked her and married her, and she gave birth to the First Emperor.' There is no suggestion of anything out of the ordinary. Nor does the idea that Lu Pu-wei fathered the First Emperor find an echo in any other historical tradition. The *Chan-kuo Ts'e* simply relates how the merchant put his riches into the campaign to raise the hostage prince to the dignity of heir apparent. Personal gain was the motive, as Lu Pu-wei informed his father. 'If I establish a country and seat its ruler, I should be wealthy enough to pass an estate on to my heirs.' No mention is made of a concubine. It would seem, therefore, that Ssu-ma Ch'ien's biography is corrupt, a later hand having invented the unsavoury episodes in order to besmirch the First Emperor's name. We know the plot of Lao Ai and the debasement of Lu Pu-wei happened, though the actual reasons are uncertain. The pregnant concubine and the extraordinary phallus must be pure inventions. They were probably employed to represent the First Emperor as being the bastard of a calculating trader and loose woman. In a society that revered ancestors the insult could not have been worse. It would be typical of the hatred directed against Ch'in Shih-huang-ti after the fall of the Ch'in dynasty for destroying traditional culture and values in his pursuit of Legalist aims.

The fall of the Grand Councillor may well have been connected with King Cheng's own views and ambitions. Lu Pu-wei's numerous 'retainers and scholarly supporters' gave the king reason to pause. Ashamed of the backwardness of Ch'in in learning, the Grand Councillor had invited 'disputing scholars' to take up residence in Hsienyang and compile an encyclopedia of current knowledge, which was entitled the *Lu-shih Ch'un-ch'iu*, or *Mr Lu's Spring and Autumn Annals*. When completed in 241 BC, this work proved to be distinctly non-authoritarian, rather Taoist than Legalist. Its views were starkly at variance with those of Li Ssu, the premier of the First Emperor after unification in 221 BC. Learned argument may in Lu Pu-wei's lifetime have already exasperated the Ch'in ruler.

Lu Pu-wei had encountered Prince Tzu-chu in Han-tan, the capital of Chao from 386 to 228 BC, when the troops of Ch'in captured the city and destroyed the state. Han-tan was one of the many prosperous centres of trade that appeared in the Chan Kuo period. The growth of commercial and industrial activities introduced urbanization as a new factor in social and economic life. A consequence was increased social mobility, though rarely as spectacular as Lu Pu-wei's rise to fame.

In Ch'un Ch'iu times, cities were more or less the fortresses of nobles who dominated the surrounding countryside from them and used them as places of refuge for their subjects during war. These cities were small and enclosed by rammed-earth walls, sometimes faced with stone. The ubiquity of walls in China has often been remarked. In fact the Chinese have the same word, *ch'eng*, for a city and city wall: town planning always commenced with external

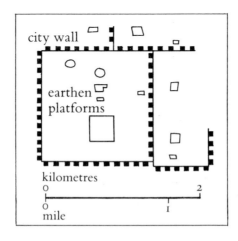

Plan of Han-tan

fortifications. By the Chan Kuo era the cities of rulers had reached a considerable size. It is estimated that Lin-tzu, the Ch'i capital, sheltered 70,000 familes, from whom the king could raise 210,000 men for military service. Archaeologists at Han-tan have traced the outline of a square city wall measuring about 1,400 metres (4593 feet) on each side. It has a base width of over twenty metres (sixty-six feet) and rose to a height of over fifteen metres (forty-nine feet). A second wall may have enclosed a smaller section of the city to the east. In the middle of the larger enclosure, located on the north–south axis, are remains of four stamped-earth platforms. On these terraces and the smaller ones dotted about the site would have stood the city's ceremonial and religious buildings: palaces and shrines. A cemetery beyond the northern city wall comprises twelve lavishly furnished tombs, five of which testify to human sacrifice.

The best excavated Chan Kuo city is Hsia-tu in the north-eastern state of Yen. The city consisted of a rectangular enclosure four by eight kilometres (two and a half by five miles) long, which was divided roughly in half by a north–south wall and ditch. The eastern half was subdivided by another wall running east–west. In the eastern sections of the city were extensive workshops manufacturing iron implements, bronze weapons, ceramic utensils, and bone ornaments. A mint also existed. Palatial buildings and houses have been excavated as well as barracks close to the gates in the various walls. In its heyday Hsia-tu was a first-class settlement, the three walled enclosures protecting large industrial, residential and commercial quarters, as well as an administrative complex. These defences bear witness to the change in the function of cities from that of a fortified stronghold to that of a regulated centre of trade.

The presence of a mint at Hsia-tu shows that money had become a significant factor in expanding the ancient Chinese economy, the barter system of the Ch'un Ch'iu period having given way to a more sophisticated method of exchange. Although gold and cloth were still used in the Chan Kuo period, cast bronze coins of several shapes circulated freely and taxes could be paid in this new currency. After unification in 221 BC the Ch'in coinage was made standard. Ch'in coins were round with square holes in the middle, suitable for stringing on cords. One bushel of grain or one bolt of silk were supposed to equal in value 1,000 of these corded coins.

The movement towards unification gathered speed after the future
First Emperor's coming of age. All eyes apprehensively watched as
Ch'in destroyed one state after another, in the words of Ssu-ma
Ch'ien, 'as a silkworm devours a mulberry leaf'. Yet even before
Prince Tzu-chu and Lu Pu-wei took up residence in Hsienyang the
scene was set for a political showdown. In 260 BC, when Ch'in
defeated Chao at the battle of Ch'ang P'ing, it slaughtered 400,000
prisoners. Having irrevocably weakened its chief opponent in
northern China, Ch'in was able in 256 BC to move against Chou and
force the Son of Heaven from his tiny throne. The intentions of
Ch'in were clear to all. They were realized through the resoluteness
of King Cheng, who guided his forces to a series of stunning
victories. Han went down in 230 BC, soon followed by Chao (228 BC)
and Wei (225 BC), but the decisive engagement did not occur till the
year 223 BC, when the rival state of Ch'u was vanquished. The fall of
Yen in 222 BC and Ch'i a year later made the 'Tiger of Ch'in', as King
Cheng was called, ruler of all China.

Chapter Five

An Age of Intellectual Turmoil

The final centuries of confusion down to the triumph of Ch'in called forth great intellectual ferment. The uncertainty of the age jarred with an increasing prosperity as cities grew in size, technology advanced, trade flourished, and agriculture improved. Rulers appeared indifferent to anything but personal gain, and only the glibbest advisers could expect to make careers for themselves and avoid miserable ends. Even a successful policy-maker like Shang Yang could find that death and dishonour awaited him at the close of his service in 338 BC. According to the *Shih Chi*, the Legalist minister received a warning of his likely fate from Chao Liang, a hermit living in Ch'in. Chao Liang told Shang Yang that his administration was loathed by the nobles and resented by the poor, that his reliance on force was no substitute for general approval, and that his own position was 'vulnerable as the morning dew'. Chao Liang therefore advised:

> *You should return the estates awarded by the king, work on a vegetable plot outside the city, and urge the ruler to honour the recluses who dwell in mountain caves, to care for the old and helpless, to show respect to elders, and reward men of virtue and merit. By doing this you would lessen your peril. If you hold on to your estates, monopolize state power, and arouse the hatred of the common people, then Ch'in will have reason enough to be rid of you once the king dies. Your end will come as quick as a kick!*

Ssu-ma Ch'ien notes that this advice was ignored and within a year the old king died, enemies slandered the patronless minister, and after an abortive rebellion Shang Yang and his family were destroyed. As a Confucianist, Ssu-ma Ch'ien believed that Shang Yang's 'falseness' deserved such a fate. It was the inevitable result of turning a deaf ear to Chao Liang, who had quoted the *Shu Ching*: 'Those with support prosper, those without support fall.' The satisfaction of Ssu-ma Ch'ien lies in the swift retribution suffered by one of the chief practitioners of Legalism. Into the mouth of the hermit the Han historian has put the fundamental precepts of Confucius, despite the Taoist reference to the ideal of eremitical obscurity.

That philosophical and scholarly advice was supposed to have been available in authoritarian Ch'in, perhaps the least civilized state in the Middle Kingdom, shows the strength of the tradition of intellectual turmoil in the Chan Kuo period as felt by Han writers. The Chan Kuo period witnessed the 'Hundred Schools', when roving philosophers offered suggestions to any lord who would listen to them or collected followers in order to establish a body of teachings. Ch'i had been the first state to encourage scholarship in the seventh century BC: it was a policy of the first hegemon, Duke Huan. By the fourth century BC the political troubles were lamented by scores of philosophers who keenly felt their own marginal influence on contemporary events. Their frustration produced a spate of speculation unmatched in the history of China. They were compelled to write books because kings would rarely listen; except for the Legalists who felt at home in the courts of hard-bitten rulers, they were obliged to sigh for the order of the world before 771 BC because conditions were not immediately suited to an alternative to feudalism. When in 221 BC the king of Ch'in completed his conquest of the other states and united the Middle Kingdom, he imposed a bureaucratic empire that left room for neither feudal sentiment nor local variation. Everything was then standardized, including thought. The reaction against this standardization toppled the Ch'in dynasty in less than a generation and inaugurated the Han empire.

Apart from Han Fei-tzu, who was a prince of the royal house of Han, the philosophers seem to have been *shih*, members of the scholar-gentry and administrative class. Their social position entitled them to a freedom of thought and movement that was denied to the noblemen above them, as it was to artisans and peasant farmers beneath them. In Lu Pu-wei's interest in philosophy during his premiership of Ch'in, we may discern the merchant's guilt about his own social and educational shortcomings. His insistence on the comprehensiveness of the book he commissioned, the *Lu-shih Ch'un-ch'iu*, was undignified at the very least. Lu Pu-wei maintained, the *Shih Chi* informs us, 'that all matters pertaining to Heaven, the earth, natural things, and to the past and the present, were contained in the work . . . a copy of which was displayed at the market-place of Hsienyang. Over one thousand pounds of gold were suspended above the text along with an offer of this sum to anyone who could add or subtract one word from it.' No one, of course, dared to improve on the *Lu-shih Ch'un-ch'iu* and risk displeasure of the self-made minister. Yet the offer of gold exactly indicated the gulf which existed between the *shang* and the *shih*, between the untutored money-maker and the learned man.

During the Ch'un Ch'iu and Chan Kuo periods four main philosophies evolved: Confucianism (*ju chia*), Taoism (*tao chia*), Moism (*mo chia*), and Legalism (*fa chia*). Although the first two were to have lasting importance in Chinese history, especially Confucianism, the most heatedly debated philosophies before the Ch'in unification were the last two. It has been said that traditional Chinese were Taoist in private and Confucianist in public, but it might be added that those who entered the later imperial service always felt the lingering influence of the administrative concepts of Legalism. The Han compromise was in one sense the humanization of a Legalist autocracy by Confucian doctrine. Only the doctrine of Mo-tzu (*c.* 479–438 BC) vanished from the Chinese mind after the First Emperor suppressed the 'Hundred Schools'.

Born in 551 BC Kung Fu-tzu, Confucius himself, was deeply attached to the feudal system. His biography in the *Shih Chi* records that he 'as a child playing games often set out the sacrificial vessels' and in his lifetime he gained the reputation of being 'expert in matters of ritual'. But Confucius' affection for the elaborate ceremonies of ancestor worship and of the court did not blind his eyes to the abuses prevalent during the Ch'un Ch'iu period. He set his mind on a course of reform, and strove for social justice within the framework of the feudal, or feudal-bureaucratic state. 'I am a transmitter and not a creator,' Confucius said. 'I believe in the past and love it.'

Though Confucius as a youth was poor (his father died when he was an infant and he was left in the care of an impoverished mother), through the patronage of a noble family in the state of Lu he was able

Facing page: An armoured archer from the vanguard of Pit No. 2. On the left is a tentative drawing of the soldier's original appearance, as made by Chinese archaeologists.

Overleaf: An artist's impression of the figures near the infantry general in the second pit.

to go to one of the private schools set up for the education of well-born children. Possibly the tradition that he was a descendant of the deposed Shang kings may have helped to give him these opportunities for learning and reading. His patrons failed, however, to secure him advancement in government service. As an official, the career of Confucius was inconspicuous and brief. The two minor posts he held were as keeper of the state granaries and director of the state pasture-lands. Confucius was unable to obtain any official appointment of note probably because he was disinclined to flatter or conduct intrigues. Temperamentally a teacher rather than a politician, he found that through his followers an influence could be exerted on the feudal courts, once rulers appreciated the value of officials who prized loyalty to principles, not factions. The students of Confucius were not chosen on grounds of birth. The only criteria for admission to the school were virtuous conduct, intelligence, and a willingness to study hard. Confucius commended in his teachings and writings the renowned rulers of former days, kings and princes whose benevolence (*jen*) and propriety (*li*) had led their subjects to perfect lives. The very character for *li*, also translated as rites, tells us a little of Confucius' original idea. The strokes represent a sacrificial vessel in which precious objects have been placed as a sacrifice to the ancestral spirits. The ceremony of ancestor worship, elevated into a moral code by his philosophy, was the meeting point of two worlds, the spiritual and the temporal. Here heavenly benefits were bestowed on the dutiful descendant, the preserver of traditional values.

The attitude of Confucius to religion was practical. 'I stand in awe of the spirits,' he told his students, 'but keep them at arm's length.' This was neither thoroughgoing rationalism nor even a sceptical point of view, but an intimation that the celestial realm was far beyond men's comprehension: something not readily plumbed by scapulimancy, star-gazing, and shuffling straws. Nor could natural phenomena, like earthquakes and floods, be so readily interpreted as the will of Heaven. Equally straightforward was Confucius' attitude to the state. When asked about government, he replied: 'Let the prince be a prince, the minister a minister, the father a father, and the son a son.' The ideal institutions, for Confucius, were those of Western Chou (1027–771 BC). The state was seen as nothing but a large family influenced by the virtuous behaviour of the ruler and the

Facing page: The statue of the infantry general. No other figure so far excavated has equalled his height.

rules of good conduct as expressed in rites. Law was unnecessary. When in 513 BC the state of Chin cast tripods engraved with a code of punishments, Confucius condemned the innovation, fearing that when the people there became acquainted with the code they would cease to respect the aristocracy, and that it would be difficult for the latter to retain their inherited positions. After the fall of the Ch'in dynasty in 206 BC this dislike of codified law on the part of Confucianists and the popular reaction against Legalist repression crystallized the Chinese view of law as something best avoided. Tradition under the Han empire was acknowledged to be the transmitter of the values of morality and culture.

According to the teachings of Confucius, the guardian of truth was the *chun-tzu*, the superior man. He is the person to whom all respond. In the *Lun-yu* (*The Analects*), when one of Confucius' disciples laments that fate has given him no brothers, a fellow student objects:

> *Heaven decrees life and death; wealth and rank depend on the will of Heaven. If a* chun-tzu *attends to his duties with courtesy to others and follows the rules of ritual, then all within the Four Seas are his brothers.*

Chun-tzu has become, therefore, a term of ethical evaluation. Its meaning in the ancient *Shih Ching* (*Book of Poetry*) was 'the son of a sovereign' or 'aristocrat'. This Confucius changed so that the word no longer referred to birth but to the qualities of a person. 'The *chun-tzu* thinks of justice, the small man of himself.'

Honours were accorded Confucius by several feudal rulers, but little heed was taken of his advice. Even his successful disciples found the growing instability of politics hard to reconcile with the humble aspirations of the *chun-tzu*. When Confucius died in 479 BC, he must have regarded the achievement of his life as of little consequence: he had been ineffectual against feudal decline. Yet through the writings of two later followers, Mencius (*c.* 372–*c.* 289 BC) and Hsun-tzu (320–235 BC), his thought was to influence the development of Chinese civilization for two thousand years. Not until the Han empire, however, were historical conditions suited to the adoption of the *chun-tzu* ideal by educated men.

Meng-tzu, or Mencius, argued against opposing philosophies, especially Moism, and propagated the doctrine of mankind's natural goodness. He was also the archetype of the filial son, the upholder of the family against the encroaching state. Whenever a ruler lost the goodwill of his subjects and resorted to oppression, the heavenly mandate was said to be withdrawn and rebellion justified. It was a democratic theory which Mencius elaborated from the famous saying in the *Shu Ching* that 'Heaven sees accordingly as the people see, Heaven hears accordingly as the people hear.' Speaking of the callousness of some Chan Kuo kings, he said: 'A benevolent man extends his love from those he loves to those he does not love. A ruthless man extends his ruthlessness from those he does not love to those he loves.' Kindness was the sign of the *chun-tzu*, who could not endure the sufferings of others. A benevolent government likewise could not endure the sufferings of the people. Unkindness and cruelty Mencius explained in the surprisingly modern terms of social deprivation. Proper upbringing was essential. The philosopher once remarked to a disciple, 'A trail through the mountains, if used, becomes a path in a short time, but, if unused, becomes blocked by grass in an equally short time. Now your heart is blocked by grass.'

Benevolent government (*jen cheng*), like the benevolent mind (*jen hsin*), was moved by compassion. The ideal king sought to nurture and nourish his subjects. He enriched the people's livelihood, levied minimal taxes, avoided unnecessary wars, and maintained boundaries. As Mencius informed the Ch'i king:

> *When a ruler rejoices in the happiness of his people they also rejoice in his happiness; when he grieves in the sorrow of his people, they also grieve in his sorrow. A common bond of happiness will pervade the kingdom; a common bond of sorrow will do the same.*

By grounding his actions in his own humanity the ruler would find the natural way of government. Mencius lamented that few kings were prepared to turn their attention away from competitive warfare: 'Never was there a time,' he said, 'when the sufferings of the people from tyrannical government were more intense than the present.'

Whereas the internecine struggles of the Chan Kuo era inclined Mencius towards ideal monarchy, with the virtuous ruler imitating the sage-kings of the past, Hsun-tzu had less patience with the feudal system and declared that merit should be the sole basis for elevation.

Unsentimental and rationalist, Hsun-tzu was prepared to compromise with the frailty of contemporary kings inasmuch that he discussed statecraft in a less philosophical manner. He was doubtless aware that Mencius failed to win acceptance for his ideas because he refused to consider anything but high political morality. Living at the very end of the Chan Kuo period and, therefore, after most of the other philosophers, Hsun-tzu was well placed to systematize the Confucian heritage as well as to apply his enormous erudition to practical matters. His thinking had a great influence on the Han empire, though in time the Chinese subordinated him to Mencius. His reputation had always suffered from the animosity directed at two of his students, Han Fei-tzu and Li Ssu. At certain points, indeed, Hsun-tzu's theories were very close to those of the Legalists, but his fundamental heterodoxy concerned human nature. In contrast with Mencius' strong emphasis on the potentiality for goodness in all men, Hsun-tzu came to the conclusion that human nature was basically evil. This initial thesis led Hsun-tzu to stress the need for education and moral training. For him the spiritual realm was a polite fiction and he poked fun at ceremonies devised to obtain heavenly favours like rain. 'They are done,' he said, 'merely for ornaments. Hence the gentleman regards them as ornaments, but the people regard them as supernatural.' Rites and ceremonies were needed by society, not Heaven. 'The ancient kings hated disorder (resulting from the self-seeking of men) and so they established ritual practices in order to curb it, to train men's desires and to provide for their satisfaction.' The ruler, a man whose intelligence and knowledge had outstripped his fellows, governed fairly and used the best abilities of his subordinates. He was 'the one who sat facing south and gave audience to the problems of government'.

Hsun-tzu visited the state of Ch'in about 264 BC. While he recognized the military and economic advantages of its rulers, he deplored their reliance on naked force and terror. Ch'in enjoyed an outstanding geographical setting: narrow mountain passes defended the frontiers of a land endowed with forests, streams and fertile valleys. Its 'simple and unsophisticated' inhabitants stood 'in deep awe of officials' and obediently followed their instructions. Hsun-tzu thought the orderliness and discipline of the state explained 'the victories of Ch'in during four generations'. Yet there were disturbing features. The absence of Confucian scholars there was matched by a lack of attention to humanizing rites and ceremonies. The Ch'in rulers, Hsun-tzu noted,

> *employ their people harshly, terrorize them with authority, embitter them with hardship, coax them with rewards, and cow them with punishments. They see to it that if the humbler people hope to gain any benefits from their superiors, they can do so only by achieving distinction in battle. They oppress the people before employing them and make them win some distinction before granting them any benefit. Rewards increase to keep pace with achievement; thus a man who returned from battle with five enemy heads is made the master of five families in his neighbourhood.*

The shortcomings of a military hierarchy later beset the successors of the First Emperor, since good soldiers often failed to be good administrators. Hsun-tzu was also almost prophetical about the overthrow of the Ch'in dynasty in his comment on its disdain for propriety (*li*) as the social cement of a civilized state.

> *Rites are the highest expression of hierarchical order, the basis for strengthening the state, the way by which to create authority, the crux of achievement and fame. By proceeding in accordance with ritual, kings gain possession of the world; by ignoring it, they bring destruction to their altars of the grain and soil. Stout armour and sharp weapons are not enough to assure victory; high walls and deep moats are not enough to assure defence; stern commands and manifold penalties are not enough to assure authority. What proceeds by the way of ritual will advance; what proceeds by any other way will fail.*

Like Mencius, Hsun-tzu believed that only a virtuous ruler could unify the feudal states. 'A petty man using petty methods,' he remarked, 'can seize a small state and hold it without much strength. But China is great and, unless a man is a sage, he cannot take possession of it.' Legalism was not enough.

The two philosophers were equally in harmony in their dislike of Mo-tzu's thought. In particular Hsun-tzu attacked Moist doctrines of frugality, social uniformity, and simple burial rites. Little in fact is known about the life of Mo-tzu, and even his writings have survived in a truncated form. He lived sometime between the death of

Confucius in 497 BC and the birth of Mencius in 372 BC. All that Ssu-ma Ch'ien can tell us is that Mo-tzu 'was apparently a high official in the state of Sung. He was skilled in defensive strategy and stood for economy in expenditures.' A Taoist tradition recorded about 130 BC states that:

> *Mo-tzo received the education of a gentleman, and was taught the ideas of Confucius; but he was displeased by the rites, which were to him complicated and troublesome; by the elaborate funerals, which were so costly that they impoverished the people; and by their extended periods of mourning, which are injurious to the health and which interfere with work. Therefore he turned his back on the Ways of Chou and adopted the governmental institutions of the Hsia.*

There is no reason to accept that Mo-tzu was a disciple of Confucius, but the starting-point of his philosophy can be seen as a disillusionment with the practice of Confucianism. Mo-tzu detested the ease with which so many Confucianists settled for comfortable careers as advisers on ritual. In this respect, his looking back to the legendary Hsia dynasty (of which there is to date no archaeological trace) was a move intended to downgrade the importance of ceremony. Ssu-ma Ch'ien said that the Hsia simply managed with 'good faith'.

Mo-tzu appears to have travelled extensively, visiting one state after another and preaching a doctrine of universal love. On one occasion he succeeded in persuading the king of Ch'u to disband an expedition against Sung. In Lu, which may have been his native state, he ran a school, and from there his followers intervened in political squabbles, offering both ethical exhortation and practical aid. Moists hastened to the relief of beleaguered states, and since many of these dedicated men were artisans skilled in the art of military defence, their arrival was often timely. Such activities have encouraged the view that Mo-tzu was a craftsman himself. This is not impossible, though the philosopher's hatred of offensive war seems to have rested on a profound pacifism rather than personal skill in the use of tools. The strength of his appeal to the contemporary mind was an understanding of fear. Mo-tzu well expressed the futility of the feudal kings' struggles. The rulers, he said,

> *set about to examine the relative merits of their soldiers, who are their*

teeth and claws, arrange their boat and chariot forces, and then, clad in strong armour and bearing sharp weapons, they set off to attack some innocent state. As soon as they enter the borders of the state, they begin cutting down the grain crops, felling trees, razing walls and fortifications, filling up moats and ponds, slaughtering the sacrificial animals, firing the ancestral temples of the state, massacring its subjects, trampling down its aged and weak, and carrying off its vessels and treasures. The soldiers are urged forward into battle by being told, 'To die in the cause of duty is the highest honour, to kill a large number of the enemy is the next highest, and to be wounded the next. But as for breaking ranks and fleeing in defeat – the penalty for that is death without the hope of pardon!' So the soldiers, too, are filled with fear.

Above all Mo-tzu was moved by the sufferings of the ordinary people. 'The man of Ch'u is my brother', he told his disciples, lest they restrict affection to family, clan, or even the purely Chinese states north of the Yang-tze river.

Mo-tzu largely blamed the feudal aristocrats and the scholar-gentry for the troubles of the period. His chief target was filial piety, so dear to the Confucianists, though he stopped short of the condemnation of feudalism enunciated in Taoism. 'The Confucianists,' Mo-tzu complained, 'corrupt men with their elaborate and showy rites and music and deceive parents with lengthy mournings and hypocritical grief. They propound fatalism, ignore poverty, and behave with tremendous arrogance.' Mencius regarded these views as the greatest threat to the Confucian concept of unselfish but carefully graded benevolence and kindness towards others. But he had to agree with Mo-tzu over the need for moderation in funerals, especially when the families of princes enclosed in tombs 'those who are chosen to go with the dead'. Human sacrifice was anathema to both philosophers.

The disappearance of Moist thought under the later empire may have been the result of the affluence then enjoyed by educated men. Stable political conditions under the Han dynasty led to a growing sophistication and rationalism, which had little interest in vengeful ghosts. Mo-tzu had argued: 'If the fact that ghosts and spirits reward the worthy and punish the evil can be made a cornerstone of policy in a state, it will provide a means to bring order to the state and benefit to the people.' Taoism was to absorb the ancient beliefs in the spirit world that Mo-tzu so ardently affirmed.

The first Taoist, according to the Confucianists, was Li Er, the 'madman of Ch'u', but it has become usual to refer to the first of the 'irresponsible hermits' as Lao-tzu, or the Old Philosopher. He may have been keeper of the royal archives at Loyang, the Chou capital, but few details are known of his life. Even his birthdate, 604 BC, is disputed and we possess no information at all about the place and date of his death. According to the *Shih Chi*,

> *When he foresaw the decay of Chou, Lao-tzu departed and came to the Han-ku Pass. The keeper asked the sage to write a book consisting of more than four thousand words, in which the proper way to live was set forth. Then he went on westwards. No one knows where he died.*

The absence of a tomb is significant; it underlines Taoist indifference to ancestor worship. The actual lifetime of Lao-tzu is now supposed to have been during the late fourth century BC, though the existence of the germinal thoughts of Taoism two centuries earlier is fully recognized.

Although the figure of Lao-tzu is wreathed uncertainly in the mists of legend, the characters in his book, the *Tao Teh Ching (The Way of Virtue)*, stand out with pristine strength. The senseless rivalry of princes is placed in a cosmic perspective. 'He who feels punctured must have been a bubble' has lost nothing of its cutting-edge in translation. Neither has 'Conduct your triumph like a funeral.' What exercised Lao-tzu's mind most was man's rootedness in Nature, the inner power that made all men wiser than they knew. 'Knowledge studies others; wisdom is self-known.' The artificial demands of feudal society had disturbed the innate abilities of men. Instead of following the natural way (*tao*), codes of love and honesty were invented to provide the people with a new social ethic. Learning became necessary, and charity was prized because sense and kindness could no longer be expected from everyone. Most unfortunate was the Confucian emphasis on the family – the preoccupation with benevolent fathers and dutiful sons. To the Taoists social evolution had taken a wrong course with feudalism. They harked back to the primitive collectivist society that was supposed to have existed prior to the legendary Hsia dynasty. Reluctance to accept office or to try reform sprang from the belief that things were best left alone. It was summed up in the concept of *jang* (yieldingness). 'The wise man,' Lao-tzu wrote, 'keeps to the deed that consists in taking no action and practices the teaching that uses no words.' The sign of the sage is effective non-assertion. He gives up in order to get; he relinquishes control in order to understand; he welcomes a relationship that is mutual; he is moved by a sense of profound non-possessiveness. *Jang* caused Chuang-tzu (350–275 BC), the most distinguished follower of Lao-tzu, to turn down the premiership of the great state of Ch'u. The account of this rejection illustrates perfectly the Taoist fear of social entanglement.

> One day the Ch'u king sent two high officials to ask Chuang-tzu to assume control of the government and become chief minister. They found Chuang-tzu fishing in P'u. Intent on what he was doing, he listened without turning his head. At last he said: 'I have been told there is in the capital a sacred tortoise which has been dead for three thousand years. And that the king keeps this tortoise carefully enclosed in a chest on the altar of the ancestral temple. Now would this tortoise rather be dead but considered holy, or alive and wagging its tail in the mud?' The two officials answered that it would prefer to be alive and wagging its tail in the mud. 'Clear off, then!' shouted Chuang-tzu. 'I, too, will wag my tail in the mud here.'

How astonished the two feudal officials must have been! The long and weary journey to the remote valley in which the sage's hut was sited would have been a trial for them, but there was the compensation that they would be the first in the court to meet the new leader. Yet Chuang-tzu had rejected an office for which others strove: Confucianists, Moists and Legalists found his behaviour inexplicable. 'A thief steals a purse and is hanged,' commented Chuang-tzu, 'while another man steals a state and becomes a prince.'

Taoism accepted neither the family nor the state as the basis of civilized living. It looked askance at the obligations both sought to impose on the individual. The need for some form of organization was admitted, but Taoist thinkers urged that it should be kept to a minimum. Of the pre-Hsia age Chuang-tzu said:

> The ancients, in cultivating tao, nourished their knowledge by calmness. Throughout their lives they refrained from employing that

knowledge contrary to Nature. Knowledge and calmness mutually sustained each other; harmony and order developed accordingly.

In the turmoil of the Chan Kuo period, the only thing the Taoists could do was follow the example of the recluse. There was no scope for the popular government that they thought had prevailed under the sage-kings of old.

Hsun-tzu was convinced that the Taoists were entirely misguided in their concentration on Nature. He marvelled that they devoted themselves to study and contemplation without ever trying to exploit their findings. He was baffled by their interest in 'things the knowledge of which does not benefit man, and ignorance concerning which does no harm to men.' Although such a detached attitude proved to be an important factor in the later development of science in China, the experiments of Taoist alchemists were by no means all disinterested. Their pursuit of the elixir of life, a chemical way to longevity, attracted the interest of numerous rulers, the First Emperor among them.

Ch'in Shih-huang-ti spent both time and money on the search for herbs of deathlessness (*pu su chih ts'ao*). According to the *Shih Chi*, in 219 BC 'the First Emperor wandered about the shore of the Eastern Sea, and offered sacrifices to the famous mountains and the great rivers and the Eight Spirits; and searched for immortals.' An expedition under a certain Hsu Fu, a native of Ch'i, was sent across the sea to 'three isles where the immortals live'. It never returned. In 215 BC a scholar from Yen named Lu attempted, with equal lack of success, to find in the mountains the famous Hsienmen Kao. The name of this Taoist adept may have meant 'Kao the Hsien Master'. It was said that he feigned residence in a constructed tomb after swallowing magical blossom. As a *hsien*, or immortal, Hsienmen Kao had achieved earthly imperishability. He was a *ti hsien*, a terrestrial immortal, who enjoyed freedom and durability within Nature. Others who were 'aged but undying' were celestial immortals (*t'ien hsien*), and corpse-free immortals (*shih chieh hsien*), whose residence was unknown. The ancient Chinese envisaged man as being made of a body joining two souls together. The *hun* soul came from the sky and returned to it, while the *p'o* soul derived from the earth and fell back into it. Their balance in the body corresponded to the universal theory of the Yin-Yang. Mention is made of two kinds of elixirs: one restrained the flight of the *p'o*, the other recalled the *hun*.

The fascination of the First Emperor with Taoist theories of immortality seems to have arisen after the unification of China. Personal contact with the scholars, adepts and magicians of the old states of Yen and Ch'i excited his imagination. In the north-east there was a strong tradition of sorcery connected with the shamanism of the steppe peoples. While one etymology of *hsien* is a man and a mountain together, the most ancient meaning of the term refers to drunken dancing and capering. It is tempting to see in these ancient revels the spirit-possessed gyrations of the medicine-man, the shaman. The non-philosophical root of Taoism was the magic of the *wu* – female and male thaumaturges. Their sympathetic magic attempted to ease the lot of the hard-pressed peasant farmers by placating malignant spirits and invoking those more kindly disposed. Details of a ceremony of exposure survive; they suggest that the drops of sweat shed by a sorcerer, dancing within a circle under the blazing sun, were expected to induce rain. The psychic powers of the *wu* also enabled contact to be made with departed spirits. Given Ch'in Shih-huang-ti's disdain for Confucianism and its ritual formalism, it is perhaps not surprising that he should have embraced the supernatural aspects of Taoist doctrines. Already in 221 BC the First Emperor had adopted the theory of the cyclic revolution of 'the Five Elements'. This also derived from a school of thought of eastern origin, and notably of the old state of Ch'i. The Naturalists (*yin-yang chia*) had much in common with the Taoists; they explained the universe in terms of the interaction of two main forces (the Yin and the Yang) as well as the play of generation and destruction of the Five Elements (*wu hsing*). The harmony of 'the ten thousand things' depended on the balance of Yin (negative, female, dark, earth) and Yang (fire, water, wood, metal and earth).

While Ch'in Shih-huang-ti's fear of dying and his anxiety about the future of his dynasty may have drawn him towards superstition, the management of his possessions remained firmly in Legalist hands during Li Ssu's ascendancy. The oldest meaning of *fa*, the fundamental concept of Legalism, is 'standard'. In the *Kuan Tzu*, the political treatise associated with Kuan Chung, it is defined as including measures of weight, length and volume. That the First Emperor standardized many aspects of social and economic life is well known, but the tremendous burden the Ch'in empire placed on the Chinese people shows how far the concept of *fa* had evolved to become one of severe regulation by an all-powerful state. The philosopher responsible for this shift of emphasis was Han Fei-tzu, who, like Shang Yang, died in the state of Ch'in.

Legalism addressed itself exclusively to the feudal rulers. Neither the hallowed customs of the past nor the private lives of individuals were its concern, except to the extent that they affected the interests of the ruling class. The only goal was to teach the ruler how to survive and prosper in the present world. Following the precepts of Shang Yang, Han Fei-tzu held that an elaborate system of laws backed by inescapable punishments was necessary for a strong state. 'If the laws are weak', he wrote, 'so is the kingdom.' Above the law himself, the ruler kept a tight rein on his bureaucratic subordinates and their activities. 'The ruler alone should possess the power, wielding it like lightning or like thunder.' Han Fei-tzu argued that the will of the ruler could be thwarted in five ways.

> *When the ministers shut out their ruler, this is one kind of block. When they get control of the wealth and resources of the state, that is a second kind of block. When they are free to issue orders as they please, this is a third kind. When they are able to do righteous deeds in their own name, this is a fourth kind. When they are able to build up their own cliques, this is a fifth kind. If the ministers shut out the ruler, then he loses the effectiveness of his position. If they control wealth and resources, he loses the means of dispensing bounty. If they issue orders as they please, he loses the means of command. If they are able to carry out righteous deeds in their own name, he loses his claim to enlightenment. And if they can build up cliques of their own, he loses his supporters. All these are rights that should be exercised by the ruler alone; they should never pass into the hands of his ministers.*

The ruler had to comprehend *shu*, the efficient techniques of administration as invented by the Han minister, Sheng Pu-hai, in the fourth century BC. 'It is hazardous for the ruler of men to trust others, for he who trusts others will be controlled by them.' He should make use of the law to restrain the authority of high officials just as he allows them to control the ordinary people. 'The enlightened ruler governs his officials; he does not govern the people.'

The contempt for culture and humanity inherent in Legalism had an influence on the First Emperor. Han Fei-tzu repeatedly called for regulation of thought. 'In the state of an enlightened ruler,' he wrote, 'there are no books; law supplies the only instruction. There are no sermons on the kings of old; the officials serve as the only teachers.' The book burning and killing of scholars in 213–212 BC was the implementation of this Legalist notion of stupefying the mind of the state. Li Ssu, the author of the first destruction, frankly advocated state control of knowledge. 'As for persons who wish to study,' he said, 'let them take the officials as their teachers.'

PART THREE

THE CH'IN EMPIRE

Chapter Six

Ch'in Shih-huang-ti, the First Emperor of China

221 BC was the year in which the armies of Ch'in conquered Ch'i, the last of the feudal states, and once the leading power in the Middle Kingdom. The fall of its capital, Lin-tzu, confirmed King Cheng as the unopposed ruler of the Chinese people, and to mark this great event he decided to adopt a new imperial title. The decision is recorded in the *Shih Chi* of Ssu-ma Ch'ien.

'Insignificant as I am,' King Cheng said, 'I have raised troops to punish the rebellious princes, and with the aid of the sacred power of our ancestors have punished them as they deserved, so that at last the empire is pacified. Now unless we create the dignity of a new title, how can we preserve our achievements for posterity? Pray discuss the question of the imperial title.'

The premier Wang Kuan, the grand councillor Feng Chieh and the chief justice Li Ssu returned this reply: 'In the past the five Emperors ruled over a thousand square li of territory, beyond which there were lords and barbarians. The distant nobles were free to pay homage or not as they pleased, for the emperor had no control over them. Now Your Majesty has raised forces of justice to punish tyrants, subjugating all the lands within the Four Seas; our provinces are everywhere and the law-codes are unified. This is something never achieved before, which not even the Five Emperors could match. We have consulted learned men and, as long ago there were Heavenly Sovereign, Earthly Sovereign and Supreme Sovereign, of whom the last named was paramount, we presume to recommend the exalted title Supreme Sovereign. Your Majesty's commands should be called "edicts", your orders "decrees", and you should refer to yourself as "our royal self".'

The king then announced, 'Supreme may be ignored but Sovereign adopted along with the ancient title of Emperor. Let me be called

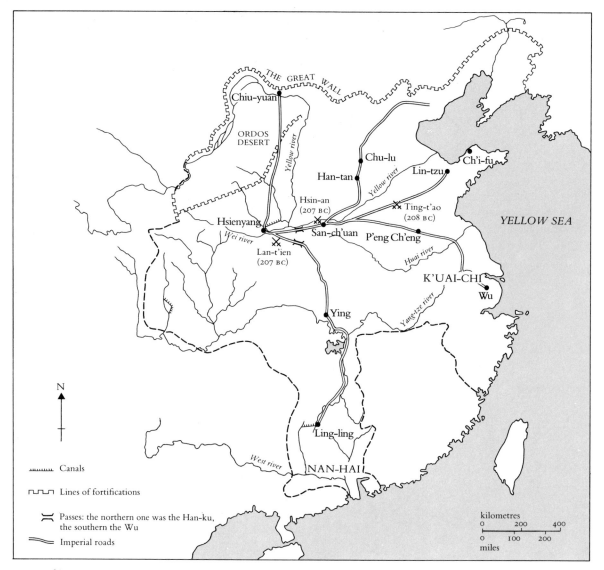

The Ch'in Empire (221–207 BC)

Sovereign Emperor. I approve your other recommendations.'

An edict was issued and the Sovereign Emperor's father, King
Chuang-hsiang, was retitled Exalted Sovereign. The edict read: 'We
have heard that in the remote past kings had titles but no posthumous
appellations. In recent times kings not only had titles but after their
death were awarded names based on their conduct. That means sons
passed judgment on their fathers, subjects on their sovereign. This

*cannot be allowed. Posthumous titles are herewith abolished. We are the
First Emperor, and our successors shall be known as the Second
Emperor, Third Emperor, and so on, for endless generations.'*

The new title of First Ch'in Sovereign Emperor, Ch'in Shih-huang-
ti, was intended to show his supremacy over the kings (*wang*) whom
he had dethroned. It may have contained the notion of divinity, or at
least divine favour. *Huang*, 'sovereign', and *shih*, 'first', are easy
enough to understand from our distance of two thousand years, but *ti*
is less clear to us because it was already an old and complex word in
221 BC.

On the oracle bones of the Shang dynasty (*c.* 1766–*c.* 1027 BC) the
character *ti* initially appears to have meant a sacrifice. The strokes
represent a bundle of burning wood, upon which the sacrificial meat
would have been cooked. Later *ti* subsumed the divine ancestors for
whom sacrifice was made. The chief among these deities was the
founder-ancestor, Shang Ti, or Highest Ti. Taking over the rituals of
the Shang kings, the usurping Chou dynasty had sought to legitimize
its authority by stressing the relationship between Shang Ti and the
ruler. The Chou king was called the Son of Heaven, and as a priest-
king he organized the state cult of the heavenly power, Shang Ti.
Well before Ch'in ended the Chou dynasty in 256 BC the decline of
traditional values had weakened the supernatural significance of *ti*,
except in one notable instance. Whereas the cult of ancestor worship,
and in consequence Shang Ti, seemed of less importance in a
belligerent world, the Taoist thinkers found in *ti* a means of elevating
the semi-divine figures they wished to claim as their own inspiration.
They looked upon Huang-ti, the Yellow Emperor, as the ancient
worthy from whom their teachings had descended. According to the
writings of Lieh-tzu, which may date from about 100 BC, Huang-ti's
long reign was said to have been a golden age. Apart from subduing
rebels – once represented as a monster with an iron head, bronze
brow, hair bristling like swords and spears, and the body of an ox,
with six arms, each having eight fingers – the Yellow Emperor
established ideal governmental institutions. He is even credited with
the invention of coined money, while his wife excelled in sericulture
and the domestic arts. When his chief minister first devised written
signs, 'all the spirits cried out in agony, as the innermost secrets of

Nature were revealed'. The renowned Yellow Emperor was one of the Five Emperors (*wu ti*) mentioned by Ch'in Shih-huang-ti's ministers.

As early as 288 BC the kings of Ch'in and Ch'i had toyed with the title of *ti*. Behind their fumblings towards the new dignity was the notion that there was room for two super-kings in China: a *ti* of the west and a *ti* of the east. In time the rulers of the Seven States came to regard *ti* as a title which could only be held by one person, the supreme monarch. When Li Ssu bade farewell to his teacher Hsun-tzu, in about 248 BC, to go and offer himself as an adviser to King Cheng he said:

> '*I have heard that an opportunity should not be missed. At present ten thousand chariots are at war and travelling politicians control the affairs of states. Now the king of Ch'in desires to swallow the world and to rule with the title of Emperor [ti]. This is the time for commoners to be busy. It is the golden opportunity for travelling politicians. . . . Therefore I intend to go westward and give counsel to the king of Ch'in.*'

In King Cheng's adoption of *ti* there was more than an element of political calculation, because the unifier of China already inclined towards the supernatural aspects of Taoism. He could not have been unaware of the manner of the Yellow Emperor's departure: after giving to his kingdom an orderliness previously unknown on earth, Huang-ti rose into the sky as a *hsien*, an immortal. Ch'in Shih-huang-ti first endeavoured to communicate with the immortals in 219 BC so as to acquire the elixir of life. As *huang-ti*, Sovereign Emperor, he fully expected to join their select band.

Yet the personal history of Cheng before his recognition as the First Emperor of China had been far from supernaturally smooth. When he came to the throne of Ch'in in 246 BC, he was only thirteen years old. The actual ruler for many years was the ex-merchant Lu Pu-wei, who had snatched Cheng's father from obscurity and secured his accession. Although Lu Pu-wei was an able minister and strategist, his regency was personally disastrous for the young king, because in 238–237 BC Cheng's own mother was implicated in a plot against the throne. The rebels were crushed, but King Cheng felt constrained to banish Lu Pu-wei who later killed himself in 235 BC and to place the queen mother under house arrest. These sombre events cast a shadow over the Ch'in court, made King Cheng mistrustful, and opened the way for the authoritarianism thereafter associated with the name of the First Emperor. The harsh dictatorship being advocated at this time by Han Fei-tzu particularly attracted King Cheng. The Legalist philosopher praised only those occupations that contributed to the military efficiency of the state. To direct all the energies of the state towards the war effort, cruel punishments were required. Han Fei-tzu argued that it has to be made worse for people to fall into the hands of the police than to fight the forces of an enemy state. Single-mindedness on the part of the ruler, he asserted in an essay entitled *The Five Lice*, was essential.

> *To reward those who cut off the heads of the enemy, and yet admire acts of mercy and compassion; to hand out titles and stipends to those who capture the enemy's cities, and yet to give ear to doctrines of universal love; to strengthen one's armour and sharpen one's weapons in preparation for the time of trouble, and yet praise the elegant attire of the non-military gentry; to hope to enrich the state through agriculture and ward off the enemy with trained soldiers, and yet pay honour to men of literary accomplishment; to spurn those people who respect their rulers and fear the law, and instead to patronize the bands of wandering knights and private swordsmen – to indulge in contradictory acts like these is to ensure that the state will never be well ordered. The nation at peace may patronize Confucian scholars and cavaliers; but the nation in time of danger must call upon its fighting men. Thus those who are of real profit to the state are not used and those who are used are of no profit. As a result, those who attend to government business are careless in their posts and wandering scholars increase in number by day. Hence the disorder of our age.*

When King Cheng saw *The Five Lice*, he exclaimed: 'If I could once meet of its author and converse with him, I should die without regret.'

The meeting took place in 233 BC, but proved fatal for the philosopher, not the king. At the suggestion of King Cheng's adviser, Li Ssu, armies had been prepared for an attack on the state of Han, the declared enemy of Ch'in since the building of the Chengkuo canal. Li Ssu told King Cheng that by seizing Han he would terrify all the other states. On the eve of the Ch'in invasion in

234–233 BC the king of Han sent Han Fei-tzu to King Cheng as a friendly ambassador. In the *Shih Chi* we read:

> *Though the Ch'in king was delighted with the philosopher, he did not yet trust him enough to use his counsel. Therefore, Li Ssu . . . did him injury and slandered him, saying, 'Han Fei-tzu is a prince of Han. At present Your Highness wishes to annex the lands of the feudal lords. Han Fei-tzu is bound to side with Han. Such is human nature . . . The best thing to do is to hand him over to the law officers for investigation.' King Cheng assented to this . . . Li Ssu then sent a man secretly to Han Fei-tzu carrying poison. Unable to obtain an interview with the king in order to state his case, Han Fei-tzu was induced to poison himself. Later the Ch'in king felt regret and sent an official to release the philosopher, but by that time only a corpse remained.*

The motives of Li Ssu are unfathomable. He had arranged the death of a man who had once been his fellow student, who was an emissary, and with whose views he himself was in accord. Possibly the two men were rivals from student days. One tradition has it that Li Ssu considered himself inferior to Han Fei-tzu. In the cut and thrust of the Ch'in court Li Ssu may have felt that his own position was insufficiently secure to tolerate the presence of such an eminent adviser to the crown. The future Grand Councillor of the Ch'in empire may have been as ambitious for power as his young master. It is also possible that Li Ssu simply distrusted any ambassador from Han, especially since the episode of Cheng Kuo, the water engineer. Whatever reason lay behind the duplicity, as a result of it the most dictatorial ruler of ancient China was tricked into allowing the destruction of the sternest advocate of totalitarianism.

Death almost visited King Cheng himself in 227 BC. The crown prince of Yen, the most north-eastern state of the Middle Kingdom, tried to persuade the scholar-swordsman Ching K'o to undertake the dangerous venture. Prince Tan said:

> *'Ch'in has an avaricious heart and its desires are insatiable. It will not be satisfied till it has subjugated the kings of all the lands within the Four Seas. Ch'in has already taken the Han ruler prisoner and annexed all his territory. It has furthermore raised troops to attack Ch'u in the south and overawe Chao in the north. . . .*

Chao cannot resist Ch'in and must accept its overlordship. If this comes to pass, then Yen will be overtaken by disaster. Yen is small and weak, and has often suffered from war. Were our entire population conscripted, the levy would be insufficient to oppose Ch'in. The feudal lords are submissive to Ch'in, and none dare join a grand alliance against it.

My secret plan is to find one of the world's brave men and send him to Ch'in, where he could play on King Cheng's cupidity. With his strength, he would certainly achieve our aim. If he could actually succeed in kidnapping the Ch'in king and force him to return his gains to the feudal lords . . . that would be splendid. But if this were not possible, he could use the opportunity to stab and kill him. . . . Then the feudal lords could unite, and their defeat of Ch'in would be assured.'

After some hesitation, Ssu-ma Ch'ien relates, Ching K'o accepted the commission. Ching K'o and a desperado named Ch'in Wu-yang were escorted to the Yen border by Prince Tan and his retinue. Dressed in white, the colour of mourning, the courtiers wept as Ching K'o sang of his impending sacrifice. 'Then he sang again,' according to the *Shih Chi*, 'a stirring song. All the gentlemen assumed a stern gaze and their hair bristled up against their caps. At this point Ching K'o went to his carriage and left. Not once did he look back.' With the two adventurers went a box containing the head of a fugitive Ch'in general, and a container holding a map of Tu-k'ang in Yen as well as a poisoned dagger. The proscribed head and the territorial gift were the bait, the weapon concealed in the rolled map was the hook.

In Hsienyang King Cheng welcomed the visitors, and at an audience,

Ching K'o approached to present the box with the head . . . followed by Ch'in Wu-yang, presenting the container with the map. When they neared the throne, Ch'in Wu-yang changed colour and trembled fearfully. The courtiers being amazed at this behaviour, Ching K'o smiled and said: 'He is a common man of the northern peoples, and has never seen the Son of Heaven. Therefore he shakes with fear. May it please Your Majesty to excuse him for a while and allow me, your humble servant, to advance.'

King Cheng replied: 'Bring the map.' Thereupon Ching K'o took

out the map, unrolled it, and exposed the dagger. Seizing the sleeve of the Ch'in king with his left hand, Ching K'o grasped the dagger with the right and struck at him. In alarm King Cheng leapt backwards so that his sleeve tore off. Though he tried hard, the king was unable to draw his sword, which was very long . . . Ching K'o pursued the Ch'in king, who ran around a pillar. The astounded courtiers were simply paralysed.

In Ch'in law a courtier was forbidden to carry weapons. Moreover the royal guard was not allowed to enter the audience chamber unless summoned. At this critical moment there was not time to call for the soldiers anyway. Thus Ching K'o chased King Cheng, who overcome by panic tried to ward off the dagger blows with his two joined hands.

At this juncture the court physician, one Hsia Wu-chu, struck Ching K'o with his medicine bag. King Cheng, however, continued to dash round and round the pillar, so distraught was he. Then a courtier cried out: 'Put your sword behind you, King!' By doing so, he found he could unsheathe the weapon and wound Ching K'o in the left thigh. Disabled, Ching K'o raised his dagger and hurled it at the king, but it missed and hit a bronze pillar. King Cheng then wounded his assailant seven more times.

Realizing his attempt had failed, Ching K'o leaned against a pillar and with a laugh said, 'I failed because I wanted to capture you alive. Someone else will now have to serve the crown prince.' Then it was that they killed Ching K'o.

A Han stone relief showing Ching K'o's attempt to assassinate Ch'in Shih-huang-ti. The emperor stands to the right of the pillar holding aloft a jade disc as a symbol of his authority. Beside the pillar is the box containing the head of the general.

The attempted assassination marked King Cheng. He 'was not at ease for a long time'. Except for Hsia Wu-chu, whom he rewarded with gold, his courtiers had hardly rallied to the defence. Anger and fear inhabited King Cheng's breast and deepened his sense of being on his own. In the biography of Ching K'o, Ssu-ma Ch'ien says 'the Ch'in king was outraged. He sent more soldiers to advance on Chao, and commanded the army of Wang Chien to invade Yen.' In the First Emperor's own biography we read that after the fall of Han-tan, the Chao capital, he 'had buried alive there all the enemies of his mother's family at the time of his birth'.

The psychological impact of this brush with violent death was reinforced after the unification of China by two further assassination attempts. About 219 BC Kao Chien-li, a friend of Ching K'o, tried to kill Ch'in Shih-huang-ti with a lead-filled harp. Kao Chien-li had accompanied Ching K'o on this instrument when he had taken his leave from Prince Tan. The musician had been blinded for his knowledge of Ching K'o's scheme, but his brilliant playing allowed him access to the court at Hsienyang. 'Immediately after the assault the Emperor had Kao Chien-li put to death, and for the rest of his life he did not allow followers of the old feudal lords to come close to him.' The third would-be assassin was Chang Liang, who in 218 BC ambushed the wrong carriage on one of the First Emperor's eastern tours. Chang Liang was seeking to avenge the dishonour of his family, members of whom were condemned to lie unburied after the conquest of Han in 230 BC. Ch'in Shih-huang-ti was unable to capture Chang Liang (who took to the hills) and 'he remained deeply uneasy'. All three assassins hurt the First Emperor's mind, if not his body. They increased his dread of dying, spurring on those fruitless searches for the elixir of immortality, and they encouraged his final aloofness from all but a small circle of advisers, indirectly abetting those intrigues so disastrous to the dynasty on his death in 210 BC.

Another near calamity for King Cheng was the invasion of Ch'u. This massive southern state posed the only real threat to the Ch'in king's plans for total conquest. Having recovered from its lengthy struggle with the border states of Wu and Yueh, Ch'u could put into the field a well-trained and well-equipped army. The iron-tipped lances of Ch'u were 'sharp as a bee's sting'. Yet King Cheng decided to entrust the invasion to a comparatively inexperienced general, for no other reason than that he offered to accomplish the task with 200,000 troops, one-third of the number which the veteran Wang Chien said were required. The mauling suffered by the expeditionary force compelled the strong-willed king to beg the old soldier for help. 'You are not too old,' King Cheng insisted, 'and you can lead the army. Grant my request, for my kingdom is in disorder, and this great defeat must be avenged by a crowning victory over Ch'u.'

Wang Chien agreed to come out of retirement on condition that the size of his army should be 600,000 men. The news that Wang Chien was to command the Ch'in invasion force quickly brought enough men to the colours to reach this total. Accompanied by King Cheng, the veteran general set off for the border of Ch'u in 223 BC. On the journey southwards, however, Wang Chien asked for gifts of land and property, which were readily granted. 'Only defeat the enemy,' said King Cheng, 'and you will never need to reproach me for my generosity.' Wang Chien then said:

> 'If it pleases Your Majesty, I would rather have gifts now. Your way of bestowing rewards is different from other dynasties. You reward men with high office which ceases with their death. Other rulers bestow titles and lands that they pass on to their children. My office dies with me, and so I ask for these lands and houses that I may give them to my children in the event of my death in the present campaign.'

King Cheng sought to reassure Wang Chien, even sending letters to him once he had crossed into Ch'u territory. By making the requests, the commander informed his officers, he hoped to maintain the king's confidence. 'In the gifts,' Wang Chien said, 'he has a guarantee of my loyalty. By rebellion I would risk them all, and by treason I could not gain more.'

The apprehensiveness of Wang Chien was probably justified. In the emergency he commanded a powerful army and he enjoyed unlimited authority. At court there would have been those who plotted against him, insinuating that his conduct of the war cloaked greater ambitions. Moreover, he knew that he could not chance a hasty engagement with the enemy. The bravery of Ch'u soldiers was well known and in defending their homes they would offer the most determined resistance on the battlefield. Perhaps taking a leaf out of Sun-tzu's *Ping-fa* (*The Art of War*), the crafty Wang Chien decided to rely on strategy. He accordingly entrenched his army in a strongly fortified camp, and there he behaved as though his soldiers had not come for the serious purpose of war, but for a prolonged holiday. They swam, sang and feasted. In the meantime the Ch'u army began to look with contempt upon the invaders. Had they not turned back one Ch'in army already? Were not the troops of Wang Chien unwilling to risk a second defeat? The Ch'u soldiers relaxed, loosened their discipline, and lost their alertness. As soon as Wang Chien perceived the moment to strike had arrived, he sent his forces crashing into the ill-prepared Ch'u army and secured an overwhelming victory. As the *Ping-fa* notes, 'those skilled in war avoid the enemy when his spirit is keen and attack him when it is sluggish and his soldiers homesick. This control is called the moral factor.'

The demise of Ch'u after Wang Chien's victory assured the triumph of Ch'in and the unification of China. The campaigns of 222 and 221 BC were the last in the series of attacks on feudal states initiated by King Cheng. By adopting the title of Ch'in Shih-huang-ti, Cheng staked his claim to be the first ruler of all the Chinese people. He was conscious of the uniqueness of his position, a lone monarch whose territories were bordered by no other civilized nation. The isolation of China from the other centres of civilization persuaded the ancient Chinese that they lived in the centre of the world. Major physical barriers such as the Gobi desert, the Yunnan and Tibetan plateaus, and the Himalayan mountain range ensured that contact between China and West and South Asia was minimal. The Great Wall, the major piece of civil engineering commissioned by the First Emperor in 214 BC, completed the landward encirclement. This 'ten thousand *li* city-wall' was more than a defence against the fierce nomadic peoples of the northern steppes. It symbolized the orderliness of China. Beyond its crenellations lay the uncivilized wastes of the outer world; inside its winding course the regulated lives of the First Emperor's subjects maintained the fabric of civilization. If Ch'in Shih-huang-ti did nothing else, he demonstrated to the Chinese the value of unity. Since 221 BC the country has been united for a longer period than it has been disunited, thus making China an exception to the rule that in the pre-modern era large states did not endure. As the first Sung Emperor was later to ask a rival who begged for independence in AD 960: 'What wrong have

your people committed to be excluded from the Empire?' It had become inconceivable that any province should seek to isolate itself: the empire was the Greece and Rome of East Asia. China was the civilized world.

In accepting the arguments of Li Ssu against the reintroduction of feudal holdings, the First Emperor evidently recognized that his reign was a turning-point in history. In 221 BC Ch'in Shih-huang-ti commented:

'If the whole world has suffered from unceasing warfare, this is the fault of feudal lords and kings. Thanks to my ancestors, the Empire has been pacified for the first time. If I restored feudal holdings, war would return. Then peace could never be found!'

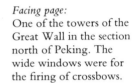

Facing page:
One of the towers of the Great Wall in the section north of Peking. The wide windows were for the firing of crossbows.

An imperial tally. The First Emperor controlled his armies strictly and only when both parts of the tally fitted together would an army accept orders as valid.

The ruthless determination that had directed the 'Tiger of Ch'in' in his defeat of the feudal states was soon apparent in the organization of the Ch'in empire. In order to unify China he was obliged to become one of the great destroyers of history. Lacking any degree of economic integration, the Ch'in empire was insecure in two main directions – the east and the north. The deposed feudal aristocracy posed an internal threat, especially in the lower valley of the Yellow river, while in the north there was danger from the Hsiung Nu nomads, probably the Huns who invaded the Roman Empire in the fifth century AD. Military control seemed the quickest and most efficient way of bringing about stability. Therefore an edict abolished feudal holdings and extended the Ch'in pattern of freehold farmers to all China. The *nung*, the peasant farmers, were simply made liable for taxes, unpaid labour on state projects, and military service. Between 221 and 213 BC wealthy or formerly noble families were moved from their homes throughout the empire to residences in Hsienyang where, isolated from their supporters, they remained without influence. In the resettlement programme of 221 BC alone

Above:
A standard measure of volume. Many of the labourers who worked at Mount Li had been condemned because of disobeying such regulations.

Facing page above left:
A standard Ch'in weight. Regulation of daily life was forced upon the First Emperor by the diversity of practices he inherited on unification.
Above right:
A gourd-like container from the Ch'in capital, Hsienyang. This is the most common form of liquid container that has been found.
Facing page below:
A chariot wheel being measured by Chinese archaeologists at Mount Li.

some 120,000 families were reportedly moved. The empire itself was divided into new administrative areas: thirty-six commanderies (*chun*), which in turn were subdivided into districts or prefectures (*hsien*). Each commandery was under the authority of a civil administrator (*chun-shou*) and a military governor (*chun-wei*). Appointed by and responsible to the central Ch'in government, these two officials worked under the watchful eye of an overseer (*chien-yu-shih*). The overseer appears to have been added to the provincial system as a means of keeping Hsienyang up to date on local developments and of checking on the implementation of central policies. The *hsien* were governed by prefects (*ling*). This centralized bureaucratic government left no room for feudalism and in a modified form it was to be the basis of the imperial system in China down to this century.

In the *Shih Chi* we read that the First Emperor had all the weapons of the empire brought to Hsienyang, 'where they were melted into bells and bell supports, and made into twelve metal human figures, each weighing thousands of pounds, these being set up within the imperial palace'. Apart from disarming the population, he also unified 'the laws and rules and weights and measures'. It was decreed that 'carts were all to be made of equal gauge and that the characters used in writing were to be made uniform'. This standardization flowed naturally from the centralization of the empire. The regionalism of the Chan Kuo period, albeit less pronounced than that of earlier times, had been accompanied by considerable diversification. Variable axle lengths, for example, caused the transfer and reweighing of goods at borders, because of the differing distance between cartwheel ruts from one state to another. An equal hindrance to trade was the variety of coinage. Bronze coins known by their distinctive shapes – the 'knife money' originally minted by Ch'i, the different 'spade monies' of Han, Chao, Wei, Sung and Yen, the 'checker pieces' of Ch'u, and not least the 'round money' of Ch'in – were not readily exchangeable. Although the First Emperor was more concerned about taxation than trade, the edict which established Ch'in coinage as the imperial standard greatly aided commercial activity. The freer interchange of people and commodities fostered a wider national consciousness but it did not excessively enrich the merchant class.

From the *Ch'ien-Han Shu* (*The History of the Former Han Dynasty*), a work dating from the beginning of the Christian era, it would appear that the Ch'in empire levied heavy taxes both in money and kind. According to this history, the First Emperor took half of the agricultural production in tax-grain, increased thirty times the tax on profits derived from the sale of salt and iron, and levied a poll-tax. Equally demanding was his use of compulsory service. In 212 BC 'he mobilized the men from families living on the left side of village gateways to guard the frontiers'. As a result, the remaining peasant farmers were unable to cultivate all the land and 'there was a shortage of food'. Requisitions of cloth also added to the misery of rural poor, whose fundamental welfare paradoxically even the most extreme Legalists recognized as the foundation of the state. During the last troubled years of the Ch'in dynasty, Li Ssu was forced to admit that the government was too overbearing. Imprisoned by Erh Shih-huang-ti, the Second Emperor, the Grand Councillor lamented in 208 BC that 'the empire was taxed heavily, without regard for the cost'.

However, the location of the imperial capital in the Wei river valley was militarily sound. From Hsienyang, protected on three sides by mountain or wasteland, Ch'in Shih-huang-ti could sweep down the valley of the Yellow river into the lowlands or retire into an almost impregnable stronghold whenever the forces of the eastern provinces were organized. A network of tree-lined roads radiating from the capital was begun so that imperial orders and troops could be rapidly conveyed to the furthest outposts. The five major trunk roads focused on Hsienyang each measured about fifteen metres (forty-nine feet) across and totalled some 7,500 kilometres (4,661 miles) in length. Lesser roads fanned out from this strategic grid, penetrating such remote areas as the upper reaches of the Yang-tze valley. One amazing route led south-west towards Yunnan, then outside the imperial frontier, and for many kilometres it ran in 'hanging galleries' suspended along the precipitous walls of gorges. Hanging galleries were wooden balconies jutting out from the cliff-face; they carried a road about five metres (sixteen feet) wide. The imperial trunk roads were policed and provided with post-stations. At the latter there were stables and couriers in readiness for the relay service, living quarters for officials and authorized travellers, and cells for prisoners moving under guard. In the method of road construction used, the Chinese had already anticipated the technique of John McAdam. Whereas the Roman road might be described as a wall laid on its side, the Ch'in road was essentially a thin, convex, watertight shell made of rammed earth, resting on ordinary subsoil. The light and elastic road surface partly accounts for the speed with which the First Emperor's engineers built a system more extensive than the Roman one. The sheer determination of the ruler must be counted as the other factor.

The resentment felt over the geographical location of the capital, tucked away in the north-western corner of the empire, was connected with the regret expressed by many *shih* over the abolition of feudalism. In 213 BC Li Ssu took advantage of the First Emperor's wilfulness to strike at this opposition and recommend the Burning of the Books. 'These scholars', he said, 'learn only from the old, not from the new, and employ their learning to oppose our rule and confuse the black-headed people . . . Let all historical records but those of Ch'in be destroyed.' Except for the volumes contained in the imperial library, it was therefore decreed that all works other than official Ch'in annals and utilitarian treatises on divination, the practice of agriculture and medicine, should be collected for burning. Furthermore, those who dared to quote the old songs or records were to be publicly executed. What the Grand Councillor feared was an alliance between the old feudal aristocracy and Confucian scholars.

He need not have worried. In 212 BC the superstitious anger of Ch'in Shih-huang-ti himself brought about a court purge. Being told by his Taoist advisers that his efforts towards immortality were being frustrated by a malignant influence at court, he decided to protect his own divinity by keeping his movements secret. Although 'he gave orders for the two hundred and seventy palaces and pavilions within two hundred *li* of Hsienyang to be connected by causeways and covered walks . . . and made disclosure of his whereabouts punishable by death', the First Emperor remained dissatisfied with the daily arrangements, especially after the Taoists quit the capital without notice. The *Shih Chi* relates,

When the emperor heard of their flight he was beside himself with rage. 'I collected all the writings of the empire and burned those which were of

no use,' he fumed. 'I assembled a host of scholars and alchemists to start a reign of peace, hoping the latter would find marvellous herbs . . . (Instead they have) wasted millions without obtaining any elixir . . . (while) the other scholars are libelling me, saying that I lack virtue. I have had inquiries made about the scholars in the capital and I find that some of them are spreading vicious rumours to confuse the people.'

Four hundred and sixty scholars were found guilty. They were buried alive in Hsienyang as a warning against further defiance of his wishes. Even more were banished to frontier areas, including the crown prince, Fu-su, who protested against these policies. Prince Fu-su had dared to suggest that such severity against Confucian scholars would unsettle the population. The First Emperor's answer was the continued destruction of all city and other local walls that could have helped local separatist movements.

It was the measure introduced to deal with the Hsiung Nu nomads, namely the building of the Great Wall, that spread dissension among the peasant farmers. This project was an immense task. Meng T'ien, the prominent Ch'in general, was ordered to set up a line of fortresses in 214 BC, but surprisingly few details were recorded of the complex logistics that must have been involved. He had already cleared the nomads from the Ordos desert and driven the imperial highway northwards from Hsienyang to Chiu-yuan in the upper Yellow river valley. In his biography of the general, Ssu-ma Ch'ien tells us that Meng T'ien built 'a Great Wall, constructing its defiles and passes in accordance with the configuration of the terrain'. The vastness of the scheme appears to have aroused superstitious fears as well as widespread discontent. Of his enforced suicide in 209 BC, Meng T'ien said:

'Indeed I have a crime for which to die. Beginning at Lin-t'ao, and extending to Liao-tung, I have made ramparts and ditches over more than ten thousand li, and in that distance it is impossible that I have not cut through the veins of the earth. This is my crime.'

Ssu-ma Ch'ien, however, comments that the general's death had less to do with geomancy than his 'little regard for the strength of the people'. In fact, Meng T'ien and Prince Fu-su were commanded to commit suicide in an edict forged by Li Ssu and the eunuch Chao Kao, after the death of the First Emperor. Yet Ssu-ma Ch'ien is

General Meng T'ien, who built the Great Wall.

correct about the harsh enforcement of Ch'in law. Literally armies of men, conscripts and convicts, toiled on the construction of the Great Wall, working and dying in the mountains and wastes of the northern frontier. Through the mobilization of labour on such an unprecedented scale, Ch'in Shih-huang-ti hoped to solve the problem of the Hsiung Nu as well as provide employment for the great reservoir of labour made idle by the end of war and the abolition of serfdom. The almost continuous use of the corvée in public works certainly did much to accelerate social change. Surnames appear for the first time. There was room in the administrative hierarchy for a new man literally to make a name for himself. But there is no denying that the apparently endless demands of the Ch'in dynasty on the ordinary people led directly to the popular uprisings that occurred after the death of the First Emperor and dethroned his feeble successors. The terrible lot of the labourers who worked under Meng T'ien is recalled in the famous legend of Meng Chiang-nu, whose conscripted scholar-husband succumbed to the hard conditions and was buried in the Great Wall. Having recovered his bones through divine aid, Meng Chiang-nu had the misfortune to be admired there by the First Emperor during a tour of inspection. Anxious above all to ensure a proper burial for her husband, the faithful widow overcame her revulsion for the emperor and agreed to enter the imperial harem once her husband's remains had been given a state funeral on the shores of the Eastern Sea. The ceremony over, Meng Chiang-nu leapt into the waves so as to join her husband in death.

Another policy of the First Emperor was encouragement of the southward movement of the Chinese people. He was anxious to halt any drift to the north in case the farmers of the northern outposts might abandon agriculture and take up stock-rearing, so strengthening the nomad economy. The Great Wall was intended to keep the First Emperor's subjects in as well as to keep his barbarian enemies out. Imperial armies first moved south against the Yueh people, who had re-established a state beyond the old Ch'u border. Next he sent a water-borne expedition up the Hsiang river, a tributary of the Yang-tze that rises on the boundary of the present-day province of Kwantung. By 210 BC the campaign had extended the First Emperor's authority into the West river basin, reaching the coast in the vicinity of modern Hong Kong. While the peoples of Nan-hai ('Sea South') were by no means assimilated or firmly controlled, they were irrevocably tied to the empire. The cutting of the Magic Canal near Ling-ling joined the Yang-tze and West river systems and facilitated the flow of men and materials southwards.

Ch'in Shih-huang-ti was efficient and hard working; he handled 'one hundred pounds of reports' daily, and he undertook frequent tours of the empire. In Legalist terms he must rank as a successful ruler. On the other hand, there was little in his reign to mitigate against the insensitivity of Legalism. His own personal drive was the engine within the Ch'in juggernaut, as his outbursts of fury on encountering obstacles only too clearly show. When in 219–218 BC, for instance, he found crossing the Yang-tze river difficult because of a gale, the First Emperor placed the blame on the river-goddess whose temple stood on a mountain close by. In retaliation he ordered 3,000 convicts to fell all the trees on its slopes, leaving the mountain bare.

The three attempted assassinations undoubtedly increased the Emperor's anxiety about dying, a weakness exploited by the scholar-magicians Hsu Fu and Lu, but the unique position of the ruler, as overlord of all within the Four Seas, also contributed to his dilemma. The concentration of wealth and prestige about a single man gave rise to expectations hitherto unknown in China. Was Cheng not the greatest king who had ever lived? Was it not fitting that his earthly reign should end in the attainment of immortality? The First Emperor's capital, palace and tomb were as lavishly planned as the Great Wall itself; and they were not regarded as extraordinary by the ruler himself. His absolute power made comparison odious. As the fugitive Taoist adept Lu noted in 212 BC, 'No fewer than three hundred astrologers are watching the stars, but these good men, for fear of giving offence, merely flatter the emperor and dare not speak of his faults. It is he who decides all affairs of state, great and small.' Yet it would seem that after the execution of the scholars that year in Hsienyang the First Emperor did leave the government more in the hands of his closest advisers, Li Ssu and Chao Kao. The discovery of a meteorite in 211 BC worried him enormously. When it was reported that someone had inscribed on the stone, 'After Ch'in Shih-huang-ti's death the land will be divided', he had the people living in the neighbourhood exterminated and the stone pulverized. 'Then the emperor', according to the *Shih Chi*, 'unable to find happiness, ordered the court scholars to write poems about immortals and pure beings, and wherever he went he made musicians set these to music and sing them.'

The First Emperor died in 210 BC while on a tour of the eastern provinces. Having progressed down the Yang-tze river and along the coast of the Yellow sea, he had a dream one night about a contest with a sea-god which had assumed a human form. In consequence he was advised to hunt a monstrous fish with a repeater crossbow, so that by slaying it he would remove the evil spirit which was keeping him from making contact with the immortals. After disposing of what was most likely a whale at Ch'i-fu, the First Emperor sickened and died within a month or so. Because they feared for their lives, Li Ssu and Chao Kao suppressed the news of the emperor's death, forged an edict ordering both the heir apparent Prince Fu-su and General Meng T'ien to commit suicide, and then forged a will entrusting the empire to the late emperor's second son, Hu-hai. As if the First Emperor were still alive, the imperial party travelled back to the capital. 'The coffin was borne in a litter escorted by the emperor's favourite eunuchs, who presented food and official reports as usual and issued imperial commands from the covered litter. . . . But it was summer and the litter began to smell. To disguise the stench the escort was told to load a cart with salted fish.' Thus it was that the body of Ch'in Shih-huang-ti, the would-be immortal ruler, returned to Hsienyang, following a cartload of mouldering fish; the very terror inspired by his own title meant that such a final indignity could happen without anyone daring to inquire. In the capital, the *Shih Chi* tells us, 'the crown prince Hu-hai succeeded to the throne as the Second Sovereign Emperor, and in the ninth month the First Emperor was buried at Mount Li.'

Chapter Seven

Li Ssu, Grand Councillor and Guiding Genius of Ch'in

According to the biography of the First Emperor, as recorded in Ssu-ma Ch'ien's *Shih Chi*, the momentous decision to extend the frontier of China northwards across the Ordos desert was reached on the slightest pretext. After inspecting the northern part of the empire, the First Emperor gave audience in Hsienyang to

> *a scholar named Lu of the old state of Yen. This man claimed to have brought from the sea a prediction made by the spirits and the deities to the effect that Ch'in would overthrow the northern barbarians. Then the emperor ordered General Meng T'ien to lead 300,000 troops against the nomadic Hsiung Nu and conquer the land south of the Yellow river.*

The *Shih Chi* thus attributes the clearing of the nomads from the arid lands within the great northern loop of the Yellow river, and the consolidation of this singular victory in the building of the Great Wall, to the First Emperor's superstitious trust of Taoist prophecy. The genesis of the northern policy in fact was more complex. As early as 300 BC increasing nomad pressure had obliged the state of Ch'in to construct a long defensive wall between the Wei and the Yellow rivers. This line of ramparts, like others thrown up by Chao and Yen, offered little more than a temporary respite in which the Seven States could settle among themselves the question of supremacy in the Middle Kingdom. A lasting solution was urgently needed after the unification of China in 221 BC, because the First Emperor could not be sure of the internal security of the empire. Nothing was more likely than rebellion when a nomad incursion tied up the bulk of the imperial forces. Meng T'ien's campaigns in the Ordos and his remodelling of existing defences into the Great Wall cannot, therefore, be seen merely as the whim of an impetuous

Li Ssu, Grand Councillor
to the First Emperor.

monarch. The northern extension of the imperial frontiers was essential for the strengthening of his newly created state. Lu's report may have convinced him that an auspicious moment to act had arrived, but the First Emperor's attention had also been directed to the nomad problem by one of his advisers, the *Shih Chi* reveals elsewhere. That person was the Grand Councillor Li Ssu.

In the biography of Li Ssu there is preserved a memorial written in 208 BC by the imprisoned minister. Addressing himself to the Second Emperor, Hu-hai, Li Ssu enumerates his own 'seven crimes'. In self-defence the Grand Councillor writes:

> *Your servant utilized his small abilities to the utmost, carefully founding laws; clandestinely dispatching plotters supplied with gold and jewels, and causing them to misadvise the feudal lords; and clandestinely to manufacture armour and weapons. He broadcast the teaching of the imperial government, promoted military men, and rewarded good officials. . . . By these methods it was eventually possible to annex all rival states, make captive their kings, and establish the king of Ch'in as the Son of Heaven. . . . He also expelled the nomads along the north, and subjugated the Yueh peoples of the south. . . . He changed harmful policies, . . . standardized weights and measures, and the written characters. . . . He laid out the imperial highways and inaugurated imperial tours of inspection. . . .*

This document recalls the major achievements of the First Emperor's reign. That such an antagonistic commentator as Ssu-ma Ch'ien includes the memorial as a matter of fact indicates how much blame was attached to Li Ssu for what happened under the Ch'in régime. Ssu-ma Ch'ien leaves no room for doubt.

> *Li Ssu went from his village in Ch'u, and entered the service of Ch'in. He used the mistakes of the feudal lords to assist its ruler and make him emperor . . . yet he paid no attention to enlightened government, never correcting the faults of Ch'in Shih-huang-ti. Indeed he was concerned to seize the greatest positions and revenues for himself.*

The question we have to try and answer here turns on the relationship between the First Emperor and his Grand Councillor. Ssu-ma Ch'ien suggests that the guiding genius behind the rise of the Ch'in dynasty was Li Ssu. How influential was Li Ssu, and how far was he able to manipulate the Ch'in ruler's own ruthless ambition?

Through his studies under Hsun-tzu, the heterodox Confucian scholar, Li Ssu became immune to the First Emperor's superstitious enthusiasm for Taoist magic. Hsun-Tzu regarded such things as falling stars and strange-sounding trees simply as natural phenomena; they were not terrifying portents. 'The sun and the moon are subject to eclipses,' he wrote, 'wind and rain do not always come at the proper season, and unusual stars occasionally appear. There never has been an age without such occurrences.' What should really be feared were 'human portents'. They occur, Hsun-tzu advised,

> when the ploughing is poorly done and the crops suffer, when the weeding is badly done and the harvest fails; when the government is evil and loses the support of the people; when the fields are neglected and crops badly attended . . . and the people are starving and die by the roadside – these are what I mean by human portents. When government commands are unenlightened, public works are undertaken at the wrong season, and agriculture is not properly attended to, these, too, are human portents. When people are called away for corvée labour at the wrong season, . . . when ritual principles are not obeyed, family affairs are not properly separated, and men and women behave wantonly, so that fathers and sons begin to doubt each other, superior and inferior become estranged, and hostile troops roam the state – these, too, are human portents. Portents such as these are born from disorder, and if all three types occur at once, there will be no safety for the state. . . . You should not only wonder at them, but fear them as well.

While the rationalism of his teacher may have kept Li Ssu on a steady course amid the increasingly superstitious atmosphere of the First Emperor's court, the successful pupil was not untouched by the grand pretensions of Hsienyang. The universal claim of the Ch'in king to be *Shih-huang-ti* matched Li Ssu's own belief in authoritarian government. Even before Li Ssu parted company with Hsun-tzu in 247 BC, the philosopher had had to rebuke his enthusiasm for Ch'in aggression. 'Ch'in has been victorious for four generations,' said Hsun-tzu, 'yet it has lived in constant terror and apprehension lest the rest of the world should one day unite and trample it down. These are the soldiers of a degenerate age, not a nation which has grasped the true principle of leadership.' But Li Ssu was keen to advance himself by using his talents, as we see from an incident Ssu-ma Chien relates in the first paragraphs of his biography:

> *In the state of Ch'u the young Li Ssu became a district clerk. In the lavatory belonging to his office, he noticed that there were rats that ate the filth, but scuttled away on the approach of a man or a dog. In the granary, however, the rats which ate the stored-up grain showed no such fear of a man or a dog. These observations caused Li Ssu to sigh and say: 'A man's talent or lack of talent is not unlike these rats. Everything depends upon where he places himself.' In consequence he became a follower of Hsun-tzu in studying the methods of statecraft.*

By the time Li Ssu had completed his education only the state of Ch'in appeared strong enough to 'give him the opportunity of performing great deeds'. Arriving at Hsienyang on the death of King Chang-hsiang in 247 BC, Li Ssu was welcomed by Lu Pu-wei, then the most important person in the capital. Through the patronage of Grand Councillor Lu Pu-wei, in 246 BC the newly arrived scholar-politician was able to address young King Cheng, the future First Emperor. According to Ssu-ma Ch'ien, Li Ssu sought to fire the ambitions of the ruler straightaway. He argued that

> *'the feudal lords already offer allegiance to Ch'in, as if they were commanderies and prefectures. With the might of Ch'in and the ability of Your Majesty, their conquest should be as easy as sweeping dust from the top of a kitchen stove. Ch'in's strength is enough to destroy the feudal lords, found a single empire, and unify the world. This is the one time of ten thousand generations. If Your Majesty lets it pass unused, the feudal lords will recover their power and will form a great alliance, against which you could never prevail, even if you were the Yellow Emperor himself.'*

Impressed with an outlook so similar to his own, King Cheng conferred on Li Ssu the office of senior scribe. The young monarch also agreed to finance the tangled web of espionage that Li Ssu was so keen to weave around the other feudal rulers. As a result secret agents were sent out to buy 'those who loved gold', and 'as for those who were unwilling, they were to be stabbed with sharp swords'. The assassination attempt of Ching K'o on the life of King Cheng in 227 BC can be viewed as the turning of Ch'in's weapons against itself.

Although Li Ssu was esteemed by King Cheng, he was almost banished from Ch'in along with other alien advisers in 237 BC. The *Shih Chi* attributes the decree ordering them to leave the state to the plot of Cheng Kuo, but this would give a date before 246 BC, far too early by any reckoning. An alternative tradition blames the reaction on the rebellion of Lao Ai and the fall of Lu Pu-wei in 238–237 BC. Li Ssu, whose name was on the list of those to be expelled, submitted to the throne a memorial outlining the benefits Ch'in had gained through employing outsiders. Swayed by the argument, King Cheng rescinded the decree and subsequently advanced Li Ssu to the rank of chief justice. After the unification of China in 221 BC Ch'in Shih-huang-ti 'made Li Ssu his Grand Councillor'.

Li Ssu's policies received a real challenge in the year 213 BC. In Ssu-ma Ch'ien's version of the event the traditionalist attack arose from a speech made by a Confucian scholar named Shun-yu Yueh at an imperial banquet in Hsienyang. Shun-yu Yueh spoke out in the defence of feudal values and suggested that a dynasty without enfeoffed supporters would find it hard to survive. He warned the First Emperor that he had 'never heard of anything endure which was not modelled on antiquity'. In reply to this criticism the Grand Councillor said:

> '*In the past the empire was disunited. Because there was no emperor, the feudal lords were active and in order to confuse the people they harped on antiquity. . . . Now Your Majesty rules a unified empire in which distinctions of right and wrong are as clear as your own unapproachable authority. Yet there are those who unofficially propagate teachings directed against imperial decrees and orders. When they hear new instructions, they criticize them in the light of their own teachings. At court they only dare to disagree in their minds, but in the streets they openly criticize your commands. To cast disrepute on their ruler they look upon as a duty; to adhere to contrary views they consider a virtue. The people are thus encouraged to be disrespectful. If this slander is not stopped, the imperial authority will decline and factionalism ensue. . . .*
>
> *Your servant requests that all persons possessing works of literature . . . and discussions of philosophers should destroy them. Those who have not destroyed them within thirty days after the issuing of the order are to be branded and sent to work as convicts. Books to be spared from*

destruction will be those on medicine, agriculture, and divination. As for persons who wish to study, let them take the officials as their teachers.'

The First Emperor approved the recommendation and the book burning took place in order to 'make the people ignorant' and to prevent the 'use of the past to discredit the present'. Li Ssu's exemption of works on divination may have been calculated, given his master's interest in the spirit world, but he may have recognized that the deeply rooted and widespread belief in its efficacy would make suppression very difficult. Apart from this, the Grand Councillor had in Legalist fashion cowed the intelligentsia. Only the ruler himself could be trusted to have a library: knowledge was henceforth intended to be an imperial monopoly.

Having undermined the position of his scholarly opponents, Li Ssu was free to press on with his programme of reforms. Ch'in Shih-huang-ti seems to have been willing to allow his senior adviser to take the initiative. In the clarification of the laws, the standardization of the writing system, the building of palaces, the expulsion of the northern barbarians, and the tours of inspection, Ssu-ma Ch'ien tells us, 'Li Ssu exerted himself.' Yet these various policies were only a continuation of the fundamental tenet of Li Ssu's political philosophy: the elevation of the ruler.

The criticism made by Shun-yu Yueh had touched upon the shortcoming of authoritarian government. The Confucian scholar had asked how the empire could be guaranteed its unity in the event of a disaster overtaking the First Emperor. He had cited the assassination of the king of Ch'i in 481 BC, the usurpation of whose throne brought about the decline of that state, and the conflict between the ministers of Chin, a bitter feud which in 403 BC led to its division into the states of Han, Chao and Wei. To avoid such misfortunes Shun-yu Yueh advised the awarding of fiefs to members of the imperial family. Together these powerful subjects could ensure the legitimate succession. He said:

> *'Your servant has heard that the reason why the Shang and Chou kings ruled for more than a thousand years was because they enfeoffed their sons, younger brothers and worthy ministers, as branches and supporting props to themselves. At present Your Majesty possesses all within the Four Seas, and still his sons and younger brothers are common men.'*

Although Shun-yu Yueh was disingenuous in not mentioning the collapse of the feudal system in the final century of the Chan Kuo period, his criticism was barbed enough to force Li Ssu to ban free thought. The Confucianists opposed the abolition of feudalism because of the emphasis their school of philosophy placed on familial relationships. Confucius had never condemned the idea of a unified empire; he had no notion of the possibility in China. It is one of the ironies of history that Confucianism was to become inextricably associated with the Chinese empire. This association started under the Han emperors, who needed for the civil service educated and trained officials untainted by Legalism. The fall of the Ch'in dynasty in 206 BC was accompanied by the fall of the School of Law. In the minds of the people, Ch'in despotism and Legalist government were synonymous, a perception not lost on the first Han emperor, Kao-tzu, who settled for a compromise in the organization of the empire. He granted fiefs to close relatives and allowed the restoration of certain feudal houses, but their diminished holdings were inter-twined with districts ruled by imperial officials. In 199 BC Emperor Han Kao-tzu even revived the Ch'in practice of concentrating old and powerful families near the capital.

The successful Han compromise would have been impossible under the Ch'in dynasty. Only Prince Fu-su seems to have possessed the intelligence to understand the need for conciliation. When the First Emperor ordered the execution of four hundred and sixty scholars in 212 BC, Prince Fu-su protested,

> '*The empire is newly established and the black-headed people in distant parts have not yet settled down. All the scholars (condemned) uphold the teachings of Confucius, and now that you are to punish them severely I fear there may be unrest throughout our land. Will you not reconsider the matter?*'

For his pains the heir apparent was sent by a furious father to supervise the work of General Meng T'ien on the northern frontier. When the First Emperor died in 210 BC, Li Ssu was party to the conspiracy against Fu-su, easily the most vigorous and able member of the imperial family. The Grand Councillor's motive appears to have been personal anxiety, a weakness skilfully played upon by the scheming eunuch Chao Kao. The prospect of Fu-su as Second

Emperor and Meng T'ien as his Grand Councillor was more than Li Ssu could bear. Because he was unwilling to risk death, Li Ssu not only acquiesced in the installation of the incompetent Hu-hai but, even more, he pandered to this ruler's insatiable lust for power. In 209 BC he wrote in a memorial to the throne that 'the intelligent ruler makes decisions solely himself and does not let his authority lie in the hands of his ministers'. This is extreme authoritarianism. Through 'the intelligent methods of Shen Pu-hai and Han Fei-tzu, carrying out their means of supervising and holding others responsible', Li Ssu argued, the ruler can 'devote himself to using the empire for his own pleasures'.

In the memorial of 209 BC Li Ssu had articulated the ultimate purpose of the state in Legalist philosophy: the ruler himself was the reason for its existence. Such frankness would have put even Shang Yang and Han Fei-tzu to shame, as they would never have dared to express their own totalitarian impulses so openly. What Li Ssu is bluntly saying is that once a ruler exercises sole power of decision, he can freely follow his own inclinations, provided his subjects are sufficiently intimidated by the threat of severe punishments. The student of Hsun-tzu had long since forgotten about the dangers of 'human portents'. It was a lapse of memory fatal to the Ch'in dynasty, as the ground swell of discontent was just then giving rise to the first wave of rebellions. 'The frontier guards of Ch'u,' the *Shih Chi* tells us, 'under the command of such men as Ch'en She and Wu Kuang, revolted and arose east of the mountains. Men of ability . . . set themselves up as lords, revolting against Ch'in. Their troops marched (far to the west) before halting.'

However, it is doubtful whether the Second Emperor would have listened to any advice which ran counter to his wishes. He was less ready to accept remonstrance than the First Emperor, even if the unscrupulous Chao Kao had allowed a minister to speak with him on matters of grievance. Chao Kao was able to deny the Grand Councillor access to the Second Emperor. When he did encourage Li Ssu to apply for an audience, the eunuch saw to it that the request interrupted merrymaking and caused the sovereign considerable annoyance. Yet the Legalist disposition of Li Ssu would have set limits on the effectiveness of his admonitions. He acknowledged the total authority of the emperor, accepting the concentration of power in one person, whatever his calibre as a ruler. The plot of 210 BC was not just a failure of nerve: the enforced suicide of Fu-su deprived the Ch'in empire of its best prince. Li Ssu's action at that time fully justified the question of Shun-yu Yueh. There was nothing to save the Ch'in dynasty – unlimited authority was bound to degenerate into excessive misuse.

Although the authoritarian empire Li Ssu strove so hard to found collapsed shortly after his execution in 208 BC, many of his policies and reforms had a lasting influence on China. The abolition of feudalism, despite the lament of Shun-yu Yueh, paved the way for the future bureaucratic Chinese empire. Immediately after unification, Ssu-ma Ch'ien relates in Li Ssu's biography, the First Emperor 'established commanderies, prefectures and townships, and melted down weapons, so that they should not be used against Ch'in. He caused the empire to be without a single foot of feudal territory, and did not establish his sons and younger brothers as kings. . . . This was done to ensure that later on there should be none of the miseries of warfare.' We know that the policy was the recommendation of Li Ssu from the First Emperor's own biography. Initially China was divided into thirty-six commanderies (*chun*), each directly administered by a civil governor, a military governor and a superintendent; the number of commanderies eventually rose to forty-two with the expansion of the imperial borders. They and their subdivisions, the *hsien*, or districts, have remained as the basic units of Chinese administration.

The succeeding Han emperors accepted a partial restoration of feudalism (in the disturbed times after the resounding fall of the Ch'in dynasty there was little political choice other than a compromise between central government and local aspirations) but they constantly endeavoured to strengthen the power of the throne. The abortive rebellion among the eastern grandees of 154 BC was used as an excuse to alter the laws of inheritance. Thereafter all sons were co-heirs to their father and land was divided between them. This amendment did much to quicken the breakdown of large units into little more than substantial country estates.

The Emperor Han Wu-ti (141–87 BC) completed the dispossession of the old aristocracy by means of harsh officials (*k'u-li*) who moved against powerful families, whether of ancient lineage or recent origin. Throughout the two thousand years of the Chinese empire the throne struggled against recurrent movements of quasi-feudal separatism, but such was the clean sweep of Li Ssu's first re-organization that it was the emperor who invariably triumphed. In this respect the strength of the central authority owed an un-acknowledged debt to Legalist theory. The administrative procedures of Shen Pu-hai, coupled with the penalties for misconduct of Han Fei-tzu, inaugurated a system of responsible government, though the emperor himself might occasionally try to enjoy the degree of despotism that Li Ssu thought possible from such an arrangement. The essential characteristic of the later Chinese empire was its bureaucracy, a ruling élite open to the talented and the well placed. Its members were overwhelmingly civilian. The most modern aspect of the imperial system, however, was the direct control exerted over daily life. Unlike the Roman model of organization, which until the third century AD was wedded to the concept of the city-state, the Chinese empire always aimed to unite and administer all its parts in a uniform manner. Ch'in centralization was never forgotten. Through the policies of his Grand Councillor, the First Emperor's unification of China equalled the political achievements of Augustus and Alexander the Great, and lasted longer.

Of all Li Ssu's reforms, the standardization of the Chinese language has probably been the most important. Although the Chinese empire suffered periods of disintegration and foreign conquest, such was the continuity and universality of the written language that political breakdown did not automatically produce cultural disunity. As with the information on the building of the Great Wall, only the barest detail is given in the *Shih Chi*. The biography of the First Emperor states boldly that 'the script was also standardized'. The exact nature of the Ch'in reform of the written language is a matter of debate, since the deliberate burning of the classics in 213 BC and the accidental loss of the imperial library in the sack of Hsienyang in 206 BC has deprived us of evidence on Chan Kuo usage. Yet the Ch'in dynasty should not bear the blame alone for the paucity of ancient texts. Before 221 BC there were feudal rulers willing to destroy any documents relating to their subservience to the Chou kings. The same impulse caused the Seven States to

Facing page: Horse's head showing a bronze bridle. The Ch'in horses were related to the Mongolian pony, larger mounts not reaching ancient China until after 100 BC.

Overleaf: Ch'in cavalryman. Notice the saddle and the plug beneath it. The latter was used by the potter-sculptor to model the hollow body.

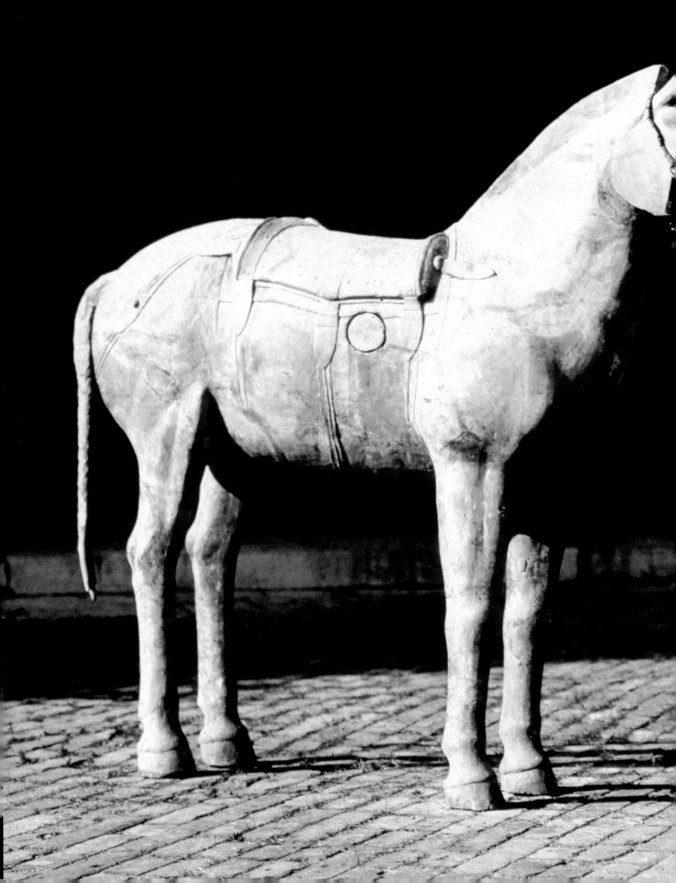

diverge in their regulations, measurements, dress, speech, and written characters.

We cannot be sure now as to the ancestry of the script adopted by Li Ssu as the standard. One theory is that the characters used in the state of Ch'in were made official and that these descended from the script of the Western Chou dynasty, which had its capital at Hao in the Wei river valley until 771 BC. The Western Chou script would appear to have derived in turn from the Shang pictograms found on oracle bones dating from about 1500 till 1027 BC. The Shang inscriptions are literally pictures of objects, actions or events. It may well be that their eventual simplification in the official script of the First Emperor confirmed the non-alphabetical character of written Chinese. On the other hand, the reform of Li Ssu could have been necessitated by the growing confusion over etymology. As early as the lifetime of Confucius there was a tendency to invent odd characters (*ch'i tzu*) when the correct forms escaped the memory. The philosopher complained: 'When I was young, I still knew some scribes who left blank the characters they could not write. Now there are no more such men!' In consequence odd characters multiplied enormously. These were firmly proscribed, along with long-cherished archaisms. The 3,000 approved forms in Li Ssu's collection probably represent a 50 per cent reduction of the characters previously used. They were called *hsiao chuan*, or small seal characters. It does not appear that the team of scholars commissioned by Li Ssu to reform the written language actually invented completely new forms. While names were obviously given to objects unknown before, by joining together elements from already existing characters, the reform involved the standardization of those natural developments in the script most suited to the needs of the empire. An easily intelligible form of writing was required for the transmission of orders and information between officials as much as 1,500 kilometres (932 miles) apart. A political bonus for the Ch'in dynasty itself would have been the elimination of forms associated after 771 BC with the Chou kings of Loyang. Their newer script was the basis of writing before 221 BC, except perhaps in Ch'in. Li Ssu did not put an end to the invention of odd characters – in the threefold expansion of forms under the Han emperors further mistakes in etymology were inevitable – but his standardization was strong

Facing page: The Great Wall of China, north of Peking. This enormous fortification was just one of the many projects commissioned by Ch'in Shih-huang-ti during his reign (221–210 BC).

enough to provide thereafter the basis of the written language. Today its great advantage to the Chinese people can be seen in overcoming differences of dialect. Only the existence of a standard written language ensures that the same edition of the *People's Daily* can be read in both Peking and Canton.

Tradition ascribes to General Meng T'ien the invention of the brush. Archaeology in recent years has proved that both writing brushes and brush-written characters were known in Chan Kuo times, but it still remains a possibility that the builder of the Great Wall also found a way of improving the brush. More certain is the contribution that he and the other Ch'in road-builders made to the integration of China, politically and economically. Reference was made to this gigantic programme of road construction in a memorial presented about 178 BC to Emperor Han Wen-ti, the first occupant of the imperial throne to embrace Confucianism whole-heartedly. The official who composed the memorial intended to warn the throne about the dangers of massive state projects. Having decried the luxury of the palaces built at Hsienyang, he continued:

> *The First Emperor ordered the building of post-roads all over the empire, east to the uttermost bounds of Ch'i and Yen, south to the extremities of Wu and Ch'u, around lakes and rivers, and along the coasts of seas; so that all was made accessible. These highways were fifty 'feet' wide, and a tree was planted every thirty 'feet' along them. The road was made very thick and firm at the edge, and tamped with metal rammers. The planting of the green pine tree was what gave beauty to the roads. Yet all this was done so that the First Emperor's successors should not have to take circuitous routes.*

We know from the Han period, too, that there was general hostility to the government officials responsible for maintaining the imperial highways. The people living near the chief roads disliked their obligation to keep the surfaces in a state of repair, to supply a tithe of food for official travellers, and to pay a special tax for the horses used in the post-service. Ordinary travellers were likewise resentful of the regulation on movement imposed by the road police, soldiers under the command of a commandant of passes and barriers who was responsible to the local provincial authorities. The road police examined travel documents and levied internal customs duties: their

Facing page:
A probable example of the calligraphy of Li Ssu. The reform of the written script by Ch'in Shih-huang-ti fixed the form for all later generations.

role was the prevention of smuggling and the maintenance of internal security. Nor was the military function of the highway system missed by minority peoples on the periphery of empire. The tribesmen of both the north-west and the south-west, cut roads and destroyed post-stations whenever resistance movements developed. Despite the memorial of 178 BC, the Han successors of Ch'in Shih-huang-ti did not neglect the network of imperial highways and the post-station system. They perceived how important communications were for a large state encompassing a number of distinct geographical regions. Their extension of the imperial trunk roads of Ch'in was instrumental in securing the permanence of Chinese unity.

Unintended beneficiaries of the improvement in communications were the *shang*, the merchants. Standardization of coinage and transport could not fail to encourage the exchange of commodities within the unified empire. Commercial enterprise seems to have intensified sufficiently after 221 BC for Li Ssu to take action against traders. An early inscription of the First Emperor reads that he 'has elevated agriculture and proscribed what is secondary'. In 214 BC another inscription tells us that 'merchants, together with vagabonds and other useless persons, were sent south'. The deportation of unproductive individuals to the uncivilized parts of the empire, coupled with the imposition of a swingeing tax on the profits from the sale of salt and iron, appears to have contained the trade boom, for a year later Li Ssu could announce that now 'families apply themselves to agriculture and artisan labour'. During the less authoritarian atmosphere of the Han empire the merchant class was able to take advantage of the increasing economic integration of the country in order to accumulate great wealth. No merchant, however, was able to use this gain to improve the social status of his family. The very first Han emperor issued an edict which prohibited merchants from wearing brocades, embroideries, silks, and other kinds of fine cloth, from carrying weapons and from riding horses. Although later rulers also levied heavy taxes on merchants' property as well as their carts and boats, the most effective curb was the blocking of all avenues of official advancement to the *shang*, because it prevented the sons of successful businessmen from taking office. This prohibition reflected the traditional attitude of the learned, the *shih*, who were determined that the merchants should remain in the lower stratum of society, but there is uncertainty as to whether it could have been enforced had not Li Ssu already moved against the *shang*. The Grand Councillor envoked his Legalist principles in the ruin of both nobles and money-makers. After the abolition of feudalism in 221 BC merchants had begun to fill the power gaps in local society, a dangerous tendency for a centralized government since funds from business enterprise could be given to rebel leaders. Once again the foresight of Li Ssu is remarkable. At the end of the Han empire (AD 220) political fragmentation was abetted by commercial interests. Li Pei, founder of Shu, one of the Three Kingdoms that succeeded the later Han dynasty, relied on the wealth of a rich man, Mi Chu, whose family had been involved in business for generations. For Li Ssu there was, of course, an example of merchant power close at hand. Lu Pu-wei always remained the skeleton in the First Emperor's family cupboard.

The reform of currency was a natural consequence of the end of feudalism. The emancipated peasantry were the source of the empire's wealth and manpower; they sustained Ch'in public works as well as its war machine. In order to preserve this economic basis the activities of the merchants had been restricted. The peasant farmers were in fact expected to contribute service, kind and money to the state. But the variety of coins minted prior to 221 BC prevented the levying of a uniform poll-tax because of notable differences in weight between them. To facilitate taxation, and not trade, therefore, Li Ssu 'made two kinds of currency . . . one of gold, and one of bronze'. Moreover, he had an edict issued which established the new Ch'in money as the imperial standard and forbade the exchange of old feudal coins or such precious objects as pearls, jade, tortoiseshell, silver and silk.

The burden of taxation and compulsory labour pressed hard enough on the population during the reign of the First Emperor, but it was after his death in 210 BC that the load became intolerable. Utterly indifferent to the sufferings of his subjects, the Second Emperor pressed on with grandiose schemes, rigorously enforced the laws, and overcame shortages in the capital by wholesale requisitions. Ssu-ma Ch'ien comments tersely: 'All members of the imperial house were intimidated while ministers who protested were accused of slander. So high officials drew their salaries but did nothing, and the common people were afraid.' Ssu-ma Ch'ien would have us believe, that in his death cell Li Ssu himself realized the mistake of supporting the Second Emperor. The tremendous taxations alienated the empire, and though at the time of this reflection in 208 BC the first rebellions had been suppressed, those unmistakable signs of break-down and disorder that were to indicate in later Chinese history an impending dynastic change were apparent. The situation was summed up by a noted Han scholar, Tung Chung-shu, who wrote:

> *The exactions of frontier military service and of public labour each year were thirty times more than in antiquity. The land taxes, poll-taxes, and taxes on profits from sales of salt and iron were twenty times greater. There were some people cultivating the lands of the rich, who suffered a tax of five tenths of their produce. Therefore the poor often wore the clothing of oxen and horses and ate the food of dogs and swine. They were burdened by avaricious and oppressive officials, and executions increased in an arbitrary manner. The people were aggrieved but had no one to rely on. They fled into the mountains and forest and became brigands. Those clothed in red filled half the road, and the number of those yearly condemned to imprisonment amounted to thousands and even to as many as ten thousand.*

Allowing for anti-Legalist sentiment and literary exaggeration by the arch-proponent of Confucianism under the Han emperors, the picture given of Ch'in repression is startling. Li Ssu must bear a considerable portion of the blame for the hardship of the ordinary people. He seems to have been preoccupied with political control to such an extent that he overlooked the damaging effect uncontrolled state expenditure was having on the national economy. Though he tried to curb the reckless speculation of the merchants, the Grand Councillor ignored the equally destructive extravagance of the two emperors whom he had served. As Ssu-ma Ch'ien asked of Li Ssu's realization of 208 BC, 'Was this not too late?'

For the safety of the Ch'in dynasty the moment for a change of policy had passed. The Second Emperor was no longer in touch with daily reality. His own relations were frightened for their lives, his most competent ministers were silenced, and the only group regularly about his person were the eunuchs of Chao Kao. From the final memorial of the Grand Councillor, it would appear that Li Ssu endeavoured to do something about the oppressiveness of the government. He lists as his last fault that he 'relaxed the punishments and reduced the collection of taxes, in order . . . to win the hearts of the people, so that they might honour the ruler and not forget him after death'. The date of these measures is unknown. If we assume that they were introduced in the reign of the Second Emperor, then the clash of wills between Li Ssu and Chao Kao may have arisen over the level of court expenditure. Li Ssu had already warned the Second Emperor that Chao Kao 'has no understanding of reason, and his avaricious desires are without satiation. He seeks profit unceasingly.' For his pains Li Ssu was arrested and thrown into prison by Chao Kao. The Second Emperor preferred to rely for advice on a man who had once been a mere palace eunuch.

In prison Li Ssu is supposed to have lamented, 'For an unprincipled ruler, how can one make any plans?' Specifically the Grand Councillor, in Ssu-ma Ch'ien's biography, mentioned how the Second Emperor 'has carried out great constructions of palace buildings, and has heavily taxed the empire, without regard to the cost'. He added:

'For the completion of the A-fang palace he has exacted taxes throughout the empire. It is not that I have not remonstrated with him, but that he would not listen to me. The sage-kings of old all had definite rules about eating and drinking; possessed a fixed number of chariots and utensils; and inhabited moderate palaces and apartments. They would never have commissioned building activities if they were contrary to the common good. That is why they ruled in peace for a long time.'

Perhaps the realization that the Ch'in empire was finished helped Li Ssu to face his own extinction, which he seems to have accepted by this time as a matter of course. Unlike Shang Yang, the Grand Councillor did not rebel, or even plot against the throne. The imminent collapse of all he had laboured for – a unified China ruled by a strong emperor – sapped his own will. What must have been specially galling was the knowledge that he himself had assisted in the succession of the incompetent Second Emperor.

In early August 208 BC Li Ssu was tortured, and then at the market-place of Hsienyang he was cut in two at the waist. His surviving son was executed with him, and afterwards his kindred were exterminated to the third degree. According to Ssu-ma Ch'ien, the last words of Li Ssu were addressed to his son. He said: 'Even if I and you wished once more to lead a yellow dog and go together out of the eastern gate in pursuit of the crafty hare, could we indeed do so?' Thereupon father and son both wept.

Chapter Eight

The Fall of the Ch'in Dynasty

Although the seeds of discontent were already sown before the death of the First Emperor in 210 BC, the Ch'in dynasty did have a chance to save itself. In the heir apparent and eldest son of the deceased ruler there existed a prince who was conscious of the need to conciliate the educated class and to reassure the ordinary people. But Prince Fu-su was the unsuspecting victim of a palace plot designed to secure the accession of his worthless younger brother Prince Hu-hai, and disaster could not then be averted. The removal of the most intelligent and vigorous member of the imperial family at a critical time left the empire in the hands of a weak despot. The Second Sovereign Emperor, or Erh Shih-huang-ti, not only proved incapable of taking advice that ran contrary to his own wishes, but even more he displayed a positive disregard for affairs of state. The usurping prince was little other than the creature of his tutor, the eunuch Chao Kao. For this reason the furious harvest of popular rebellions which started in 208 BC toppled the Ch'in dynasty from the imperial throne.

The involvement of Li Ssu in the plot to make Hu-hai the Second Emperor weakened the influence of the elder statesman on the young ruler. Erh Shih-huang-ti was only twenty-one years old. By making Li Ssu an accomplice, Chao Kao cleverly ensured that there was no one who could challenge his own position. It would appear that the Second Emperor was emotionally dependent on the eunuch, who 'had taught Hu-hai writing and the legal codes'. From the moment the conspiracy was launched the prince effectively committed himself to 'Chao Kao and five or six other trusted eunuchs'. With the assistance of Li Ssu, this group achieved an unopposed palace coup and inaugurated the reign of Erh Shih-huang-ti, a ruler in a line the

First Emperor had proclaimed would last for 'endless generations'. In the event he ruled for barely three years; his successor, Tzu-ying, lasted for less than two months. When in 206 BC Liu Pang, the future Han emperor Kao-tsu, marched his rebel army through the Wu pass, it was as the Ch'in king and not the Third Sovereign Emperor that Tzu-ying surrendered. The nephew of the Hu-hai had not dared to assume the imperial title. With 'a cord round his neck, the imperial seal and tally in his hands, Tzu-ying drove out in a plain carriage with white horses to surrender'.

Having buried his father along with the childless members of the imperial harem, as well as the artisans who constructed the great tomb at Mount Li, Erh Shih-huang-ti toured the eastern parts of the empire in the spring of 209 BC. On his return to Hsienyang, according to the account given by Ssu-ma Ch'ien at the end of his biography of the First Emperor, Erh Shih-huang-ti complained to Chao Kao about the number of persons who dared to opposed his will.

> *The Second Emperor said: 'The leading ministers question my policy, the officials possess much power, and the princes are bound to contest my authority. What shall I do?'*
>
> *In reply, his chamberlain Chao Kao said: 'The leading ministers of the last emperor came from families famous throughout the land for generations, whose feats are well remembered. I am humble and obscure, yet Your Majesty graciously raised me up to hold high office and order affairs in the palace. This has annoyed the chief ministers, who only pretend to obey me but at heart are resentful. If you seize this chance to make an example of those provincial officials, civil and military, whose crimes you discovered during your tour of inspection, you will frighten the empire and remove those who oppose us. This is no moment for gentleness. Strength is required. I implore you to act swiftly before these officials have time to conspire, so that as a wise ruler you win over the rest of your subjects, ennobling the humble, enriching the poor and making the distant close. Then high and low will rally round you and the empire will be secure.'*

Erh Shih-huang-ti took this advice. 'He sentenced leading ministers and princes to death and had accusations brought against those close to his person.' Exact details of the purge are hard to find, though Ssu-ma Ch'ien refers to the killings in several chapters of the *Shih Chi*.

Certainly a number of ministers at Hsienyang were executed and the bodies of princes were also exposed in the market-place there. At nearby Tu, 'ten of the princesses of the imperial family were killed by being torn limb from limb'. One of Ch'in Shih-huang-ti's sons requested funds to pay for his own funeral at the foot of Mount Li, since he preferred to follow his father to the grave. The Second Emperor was delighted, exclaiming to Chao Kao: 'This request is prompt!' One hundred thousand coins were immediately granted for the funeral expenses. Other victims included members of the armed forces, three captains of the Imperial Guards being removed from their posts.

What role Li Ssu played in all this is uncertain. Ssu-ma Ch'ien implies that the Second Emperor consulted secretly only with Chao Kao. There is some evidence, as we saw, to suggest that Li Ssu tried to ease the repression under the Second Emperor, but his own prejudice in favour of dictatorship would have severely limited the extent of his dissent. In his biography of Li Ssu, however, Ssu-ma Ch'ien advances a personal reason for the lack of protest. His eldest son, Li Yu, administrator of San Ch'uan, had been unable to prevent a group of rebels from passing through. Under the Ch'in system of official responsibility Li Yu was culpable, and therefore Li Ssu 'assented to the Second Emperor's ideas, hoping in this way to obtain favour'. Of course the Grand Councillor no longer enjoyed an intimate relationship with the throne. Whereas Ch'in Shih-huang-ti seems to have taken him into the closest confidence, Erh Shih-huang-ti refused to grant audiences and 'made reproving inquiries of Li Ssu'. The exclusion of the minister was doubtless the work of Chao Kao, who in 208 BC engineered Li Ssu's disgrace and death. The growing power of the eunuch became apparent to all in the previous year when the Second Emperor was persuaded to keep to the inner palace. Chao Kao had told his sovereign that

> 'What makes the Son of Heaven appear noble in the eyes of his people is that they hear only the sound of his voice, no one ever being able to gaze on his countenance. Thus he rightly refers to himself as an immortal. Furthermore, Your Majesty has yet many years to rule, and is not yet necessarily conversant with all matters of state. If now you were to sit in court and some mistake were to occur in the proceedings,

179

you would show your shortcomings to the leading ministers, instead of displaying your spirit-like intelligence to the empire. If on the other hand you reserved your dignity within the forbidden parts of the palace, and you leave it to me and to the palace attendants practised in the laws to handle matters when they arise, then there would be someone to make a decision, so that the ministers would refrain from bringing up unnecessary matters and the empire would acclaim Your Majesty a sage ruler.'

'Unnecessary matters' were unwelcome tidings such as the rebellion of Ch'en She in the Yang-tze river valley. A farmhand threatened with death for disobedience, Ch'en She had become the focus of the first popular movement against the Ch'in empire. Although the insurrection rapidly spread northwards and attracted 'untold numbers of young men', the Second Emperor characteristically struck out at the easiest target on hearing the news. 'Erh Shih-huang-ti in a rage committed the messenger to trial.' As a result the next messenger to arrive in Hsienyang informed the emperor that the belligerents 'were bands of brigands, now all captured by the forces sent by local governors. There is no cause for alarm.' Yet the increasing boldness of the rebels compelled the Second Emperor to admit that action was necessary and 'in great dismay he took counsel with his ministers'. The military situation of the capital was so desperate that it was decided to adopt the plan of Chang Han, an official of the revenue department. Chang Han urged that 'because the rebel army is strong and at hand, and troops cannot be summoned in time from elsewhere, the many conscripts on Mount Li should be pardoned and armed'. Erh Shih-huang-ti agreed and appointed Chang Han commander of the new force. Quite possibly some of the weapons carried by these men so hastily assembled in the emergency came from the pits of the pottery army.

Chang Han's ex-convicts acquitted themselves well in battle, routing the forces of Ch'en She (who died at the hand of a treacherous follower) and pursuing the remnants of his army eastwards. Though his attempted rebellion of 209 BC had failed, he was the spark that lit the prairie fire of widespread peasant revolt. 'Uprisings increased and troops had to be sent again and again from within the Pass to attack the rebels in the east.' The first Han emperor,

Kao-tsu, later acknowledged his debt to Ch'en She by establishing thirty families near his grave in order that the first rebel leader might enjoy regular sacrifices.

Saved from immediate danger, Erh Shih-huang-ti soon relapsed into indolence within the inner palace, leaving the day-to-day running of the empire to Chao Kao and his eunuchs. Immediate security at Hsienyang was provided by a special garrison of 50,000 picked men, whose extra mouths added to the burden on the surrounding countryside. Aware that even this addition to the population of the capital was increasing an intolerable strain, ministers Feng Chu-chi and Li Ssu and General Feng Chieh presented this memorial to the emperor:

> *Brigands swarm east of the Pass. Although the imperial forces have
> dealt with a great many of these robbers, they are still not yet wiped out.
> The cause of all this disorder is the bitter load of garrison duty,
> construction work, transport service, and heavy taxation borne by the
> people. We propose calling a halt to the work on the A-fang palace, and
> a reduction of transport duties and garrison service.*

Already poisoned against Li Ssu by the slanders of Chao Kao – he claimed that the Grand Councillor hoped to become a king on the partition of the empire – Erh Shih-huang-ti replied in the following terms:

> '*What is splendid about possessing an empire is being able to do as you
> please and satisfy your desires. By placing emphasis on clearly
> understood laws, a ruler can prevent his subjects from behaving badly
> and so control the land within the Four Seas. . . . In name we are lord of
> ten thousand chariots, but not in fact. Thus I want a retinue of not a
> thousand but ten thousand chariots to match my title.*
>
> *My father began as the king of a single state, yet he founded the
> empire. He repelled the barbarians, pacified the country, and built
> palaces to mark his success. You saw these achievements. Now during
> the two years of my reign brigands have been making trouble on all
> sides, yet you urge me to give up my father's tasks. You are neither
> carrying out the wishes of the First Emperor nor are you working
> loyally for me. You are unfit for office!*'

Arrested for their expression of concern, Feng Chu-chi and Feng

Chieh chose suicide rather than public disgrace, while Li Ssu was tortured and executed. The removal of these men left Chao Kao without a rival at court.

Meanwhile Chang Han had spent 208 BC campaigning against the rebels. But neither the death of Ch'en She nor the continued successes of Chang Han could quench the flames of the rebellion. Ambitious men outside the Ch'in passes saw their opportunity, excited their neighbours to attack imperial officials, and put themselves at the head of a rebel force. Such a rebel leader was Hsiang Yu, who with his uncle Hsiang Liang decapitated the Ch'in governor of K'uai-chi, the commandery in the lower Yang-tze valley. Not only had the noble Hsiang family often provided generals for the old state of Ch'u, but the physical presence of Hsiang Yu also commanded respect. In his biography Ssu-ma Ch'ien tells us that he was 'so strong he could lift a bronze cauldron with two hands'. As the Hsiang rebel army moved northwards other rebel leaders came to join forces with it, one of these being Liu Pang, the future first emperor of the Han dynasty. While Liu Pang was sent westwards to take the war to Hsienyang itself, Hsiang Liang grew over-confident of his strength and risked an engagement at Ting-t'ao with Chang Han, whose convict army was now reinforced by all the reserves of Ch'in. The action closed with an overwhelming victory for Chang Han and a miserable death for Hsiang Liang.

Through a mixture of courage and cunning, Hsiang Yu managed to reassert the family leadership after this resounding defeat and take command of the main rebel army. It was his determination which gained him a potent reputation. When in 207 BC, on the way to lift the siege of Chu-lu, Hsiang Yu crossed the Yellow river, he 'sank all his boats, smashed the cooking pots and vessels, and set fire to his huts, to make clear to his soldiers that they must fight to the death, for he had no intention of retreating'. After nine battles Hsiang Yu put the imperial forces besieging Chu-lu to flight. The moment to redeem his uncle's defeat had come. Turning towards the south-west Hsiang Yu made contact with Chang Han, but for several weeks they manœuvred their armies without engaging in battle. The Ch'in army had on more than one occasion been forced to retreat, and the Second Emperor sent an envoy to reprimand Chang Han for this. Ssu-ma Ch'ien writes:

'In alarm Chang Han dispatched his secretary Ssu-ma Hin to ask instructions from Chao Kao, then the prime minister. But Chao Kao would not see him or believe his account. Fearful for his own safety, Ssu-ma Hin fled and the men Chao Kao sent in pursuit failed to overtake him. Back at Chang Han's camp Ssu-ma Hin said: 'Chao Kao is now in charge at court. Whether you win or lose, you will be condemned.'

Perplexed and unnerved by this information, Chang Han secretly opened negotiations with the rebels on the possibility of an alliance between the two armies. Though Hsiang Yu would have preferred to settle the issue on the battlefield, the exhaustion of his supplies dictated a softer approach and so Chang Han, 'with tears streaming from his eyes', joined the rebels and was made king of Yung. To Ssu-ma Hin, Hsiang Yu gave the command of the Ch'in forces as well as orders to advance as far as the city of Hsin-an. This the new commander did with difficulty. His men were much abused by the rebels, who before as workers on construction projects or as guards on garrison duty had themselves been ruthlessly treated by the officers and men of Ch'in. Discontent among the ranks of the Ch'in army at Hsin-an grew loud and was reported to Hsiang Yu. In order to forestall an independent move by Ssu-ma Hin's men into the Wei river valley Hsiang Yu ordered his army to make a surprise attack on them by night. Two hundred thousand men were butchered, about the same number of casualties as already sustained by the imperial forces during the two-year campaign of Chang Han. The Hsin-an massacre ended Ch'in military power. It occurred just fifty-three years after Ch'in had slaughtered twice as many Chao prisoners following the battle of Ch'ang P'ing.

While the imperial forces outside the ancient boundaries of Ch'in were being annihilated by the rebels under Hsiang Yu, a bizarre series of events at Hsienyang itself delivered up the dynasty and all its treasures to the south-eastern attack of Liu Pang. Once again the blame lies with Chao Kao. The *Shih Chi* offers us two lengthy versions of the surreal happenings, one in Li Ssu's biography and the other in the First Emperor's. By putting these together we can obtain a continuous narrative. Having disposed of Li Ssu and assumed the title of Grand Councillor, Chao Kao, eager for more power still, 'made a test to see if the officials would obey him or not'.

> On 27 September 207 BC, Chao Kao presented a stag to the Second
> Emperor, all the time calling the animal a horse. With a laugh the
> emperor said, 'Are you not mistaken, prime minister? This is a stag,
> not a horse.' But when the Second Emperor appealed to the officials
> present, some remained silent, many said it was a horse to please Chao
> Kao, and only a few agreed it was a stag. Later Chao Kao secretly
> impeached and punished those who had dared to say it was a stag, after
> which all the officials were afraid of him.
>
> As a consequence of this presentation, the Second Emperor thought he
> was suffering from a delusion. In alarm he summoned the Great Diviner
> to explain the matter. The Great Diviner said: 'When performing the
> suburban sacrifices in spring and autumn as well as making offerings in
> the ancestral temple and to the immortals and spirits, Your Majesty has
> not been pure in his fasting, and that is why he has come to this. He
> should depend on his abundant virtue and be strict about his fasts.'
>
> Then the Second Emperor went to Shang-lin park to fast. There he
> went out hunting every day. On one occasion there was a stranger in the
> park grounds, a traveller, and the Second Emperor shot an arrow and
> killed him. Whereupon Chao Kao instructed his son-in-law Yen Lo,
> the governor of Hsienyang, to bring charges against the murderer
> irrespective of his rank. (Yen Lo was probably the husband of a
> daughter adopted by the eunuch.) Chao Kao himself also reproved the
> emperor with these words: 'The Son of Heaven has slain an innocent
> man without any justification at all. Heaven forbids such a crime and
> the spirits will now reject your sacrifices. Calamities will pour down
> upon us. You must go away from the capital in order to make a special
> sacrifice – to ward off the evil.'
>
> The Second Emperor then went to the Wang-i palace, a short
> distance from Hsienyang. Already he had been disturbed and puzzled
> by a strange dream in which a white tiger killed the left horse of his
> carriage. This was interpreted as an evil influence at work in the Wei
> river. So the Second Emperor purified himself in the Wang-i palace and
> prepared to sacrifice to the river-god by drowning four white horses in
> the waters. He also sent a messenger to reprimand Chao Kao for not
> suppressing the rebels. Alarmed by this message, Chao Kao plotted with
> Yen Lo and Chao Cheng, his younger brother.

'*The emperor never takes good advice,*' *Chao Kao informed them.*
'*In the present crisis he intends to hold us responsible. I would like to*
instal Prince Tzu-ying in his place, for Tzu-ying is kindly and modest.
He has always made a favourable impression on the people.'

The conspirators enlisted the aid of the chamberlain of Wang-i
palace, who announced that rebels had broken into the building and
ordered Yen Lo to bring officers and troops to seize them. Holding Yen
Lo's mother in his house as a hostage, Chao Kao dispatched him with a
thousand men to the gate of Wang-i palace. There the captain of the
detachment guarding the Second Emperor was beheaded by Yen Lo,
who forcibly entered the palace, his men discharging arrows as they
went. Guards and eunuchs were quickly overpowered, a dozen or so
being killed. Then the chamberlain led Yen Lo to the throne room,
where arrows were shot at the hangings of the throne. Angrily the
Second Emperor shouted for help, but only one eunuch was brave
enough to stay beside him. Turning to his lone companion, the emperor
asked, 'Why didn't you speak out earlier, before it came to this?' He
replied: 'My life was spared because I did not dare to utter a word. Had
I spoken before, I would already be in my grave now.'

Approaching the ruler Yen Lo denounced him as a tyrant and a
heartless executioner. 'The whole world is against you,' he cried.
'*Choose how you wish to die.*'

'*May I speak to the prime minister?*' *asked the Second Emperor.*
'*No,*' *answered Yen Lo.*
'*I will be the lord of a province*', *offered the Second Emperor.*
'*No,*' *answered Yen Lo again.*
'*Let me live*', *pleaded the Second Emperor* '*with my wife and*
children as an ordinary citizen like the other princes.'
'*I am charged*', *replied Yen Lo, 'by the prime minister to execute you*
on behalf of the entire empire. Whatever you say will not matter one
jot.' As he called in his men, the Second Emperor killed himself.

This version of the death of Erh Shih-huang-ti is somewhat different
from that given in Li Ssu's biography. In the latter there is no hint of
Chao Kao's terrorism amongst his own relations. Neither Yen Lo
nor his hostage mother appear. The enforced suicide is represented as
part of an attempted usurpation of the throne by the prime minister
himself. Before giving in full this other account of the events of

12–13 October 207 BC, there are important details to note in the one above. The eunuch who remained with the Second Emperor knew of the conspiracy beforehand. Either he was party to it or he was unable to find anyone in Hsienyang capable of stopping the plotters. The stranglehold of Chao Kao on the capital after the incident of the stag must have been complete. Yen Lo controlled the forces of law and order and could even presume to worry the ruler himself with a prosecution for murder. Moreover, the men directly under his authority as governor were adequate to intimidate the emperor's personal bodyguard. That his father-in-law held Yen Lo's own mother as a precaution against double-dealing indicates how much Chao Kao's eminence rested on naked terror. Chao Kao exploited others through their fears, whether they were related to him or not. In the version of the Second Emperor's death given in the biography of Li Ssu it is Chao Kao who plays the leading part. We read:

> *After the Second Emperor had been at Wang-i palace for three days, Chao Kao summoned the guard and commanded the soldiers to put on ordinary clothes. He then entered the palace and told the Second Emperor that bandits had arrived from the mountains. Having mounted a pavilion, the Second Emperor saw the soldiers (dressed in ordinary clothes) and was overcome by fear. Chao Kao seized the chance to force him to commit suicide. Then Chao Kao took the imperial seal and hung it from his own belt. But no official would accept his usurpation, and when he ascended the audience hall, three persons there offered him harm. Realizing that Heaven had refused to grant him the empire, and that the officials as a whole would not co-operate with his desire, he summoned a nephew of the late emperor and handed over the imperial seal.*

The bid for absolute power having ended in failure, and the accession of a member of the imperial clan being assured, Chao Kao strove to maintain his own position as best he could. As prime minister he addressed the leading ministers and princes in these words:

> *'Ch'in was formerly a state. Not until he became ruler of all the states in the Middle Kingdom did the First Emperor assume the imperial title. Now that these states have reasserted their independence and our territory has shrunk accordingly it would be improper to retain an empty imperial dignity. Let us rather have a king as before.'*

*So it was that Tzu-ying, the son of one of the Second Emperor's
elder brothers, was proclaimed as the Ch'in king. The Second Emperor
was buried like a common citizen south of Tu. Then Chao Kao
requested Tzu-ying to fast for a certain number of days prior to
attending the ancestral temple in order to receive formally the royal seal.
After five days Tzu-ying told his sons of his anxieties concerning the
prime minister. He said:*

*'Chao Kao murdered the Second Emperor at Wang-i palace. Because
he could not win over the other officials he has pretended to enthrone me.
I have heard that he has agreed with the rebels to destroy the house of
Ch'in in return for becoming himself the prince within the Pass. I
believe the ceremony he has planned in the ancestral temple will end
with my death there. I am going to feign illness so that he visits us here.
Then I shall kill him.'*

*When Chao Kao came at last to inquire about the king's illness,
Tzu-ying had another eunuch named Han T'an stab the prime minister
to death. Afterwards Chao Kao's kindred were exterminated to the third
degree.*

*Tzu-ying sat on the throne for only forty-six days. In early February
206 BC the soldiers of the duke of P'ei (Liu Pang) reached Hsienyang
via the Wu pass. Ministers and princes forgot their duties and
surrendered to the rebels. In consequence Tzu-ying, accompanied by his
wife and sons, bound his neck with a silken cord and made his
submission at Chih -tao, south-east of Hsienyang. Thereupon the duke
took charge of the king and his capital, sealing up the treasures and
palaces. He pitched his camp at Pa-shang. More than a month later
Hsiang Yu arrived with the main rebel army of 400,000 men. Then
Tzu-ying was beheaded along with all the other members of the
imperial clan. Indeed there was a massacre in Hsienyang. Palaces and
houses were looted and fired. The burning did not cease until the third
month. Thus it is that the Ch'in empire was lost.*

The violence of March or April 206 BC was unprecedented. The
conflagration engulfed the imperial collection of books, in many
cases the sole surviving copies. This second Burning of the Books
destroyed the intellectual heritage of feudalism in a more thorough
way than ever Li Ssu had dreamed was possible. It caused a definite
break in consciousness. When, in Han times, the ancient texts were

painfully reconstructed from memory and the badly tattered copies that had been hidden in 213 BC at great personal risk were unearthed, the feudal world seemed historically remote. If Li Ssu broke the power of the feudal nobles, it was the enraged peasant army of Hsiang Yu that obliterated their culture. The semi-feudal compromise of the Han dynasty – which Ssu-ma Ch'ien says was founded five years after the sack of Hsienyang – did not turn the clock back to the era before 221 BC. On the contrary, the Han empire represented the accommodation of local separatism within the structure of a centralized state. Its founder actually dated the beginning of his reign from the day Tzu-ying submitted to him at Chih-tao.

Liu Pang (already made the duke of P'ei by Hsiang Yu) had been offered a share of the Land within the Passes by Chao Kao, after the death of the Second Emperor. Guessing correctly that this was only a ploy, Liu Pang forced the Wu pass and at Lan-t'ien inflicted a heavy reverse on the Ch'in forces sent against him. His mildness to the people of Ch'in – 'whenever he passed', Ssu-ma Ch'ien says in his biography, 'he forbade his men to plunder or take captives' – contrasted with the ferocity of Hsiang Yu, then the acknowledged commander-in-chief of the rebel armies. Everywhere Liu Pang went there was praise for his actions; he treated his men fairly and generously, showed mercy to his enemies, and expressed a genuine concern for the well-being of the people. In 206 BC the devastation of the Ch'in capital and the subsequent division of the empire between the rebel leaders were beyond his prevention. In 203 BC Liu Pang felt obliged to upbraid Hsiang Yu for his misbehaviour. 'You fired the palaces of Ch'in', he said. 'You desecrated the tomb of the First Emperor and you appropriated the wealth and goods of Ch'in for your private use. . . . You executed Tzu-ying, the king of Ch'in, who had already surrendered.' What made this arrogance on the part of Hsiang Yu more than he could stomach was the breaking of the agreement by the rebel leaders that whoever took Hsienyang should become king of Ch'in. Liu Pang had been created in 206 BC king of Han, an area comprising only the northern portions of the Ch'in territories of Shu and Pa.

Conflict between Hsiang Yu and Liu Pang was unavoidable. These two remarkable men had nothing but ambition in common. Hsiang Yu, a descendant of the old Ch'u nobility, had informed his

Facing page:
The destruction of the pits containing the terracotta army at Mount Li was caused by the peasant rebel army in 206 BC.

uncle Hsiang Liang during one of the First Emperor's tours of K'uai-chi that, 'the fellow could be deposed and replaced!'; while the peasant Liu Pang (originally Liu Chi), on a tour of garrison duty in Hsienyang, had said of the same ruler, 'Ah! A real man should be like this.' Liu Pang had to wait for the arrogance and cruelty of Hsiang Yu to alienate his supporters. One immediate advantage he enjoyed was proximity to the Wei river valley, an area Hsiang Yu foolishly handed over to three ex-Ch'in generals who had surrendered along with Chang Han. The *Shih Chi* records the shortsightedness of this decision.

> *Someone advised Hsiang Yu, saying: 'The Land within the Passes is on all four sides protected by barriers of mountains and rivers, and the soil is rich and fertile. Here you should place your capital and rule as dictator.' But Hsiang Yu, seeing that the palaces of Ch'in were no more and remembering his native place, determined to leave. He said: 'To become wealthy and famous and then to not return home is like putting on an embroidered coat and walking about in the dark. Who would know about it?'*
>
> *Later the man who advised him remarked that he now understood the saying that, 'The men of Ch'u are monkeys with hats on.' When this was reported to Hsiang Yu he had the adviser boiled alive.*

Liu Pang struck within a month of Hsiang Yu's departure. In September 206 BC he overran the Wei river valley and fortified the Wu and Han-ku passes. Hsiang Yu was furious at the news but also found himself having to deal with opposition closer to his own capital of P'eng Ch'eng. His army was committed to an attack on the ruler of Ch'i, whose notions of independence he disliked thoroughly. Though the excesses of his troops in this campaign shocked his brother monarchs and roused the inhabitants of Ch'i to further resistance, the position of Hsiang Yu was weakened most by the news of his assassination of the 'Righteous Emperor', the king of Ch'u. This insignificant ruler had been set up by the rebels at the beginning of the revolt as their nominal Son of Heaven. In May 205 BC Liu Pang led five other kings in a crusade against P'eng Ch'eng, the army under his command being 560,000 strong. Hsiang Yu smashed this force with a much smaller number of crack troops on the banks of the Sui river, a few kilometres east of his capital. The *Ch'ien-Han Shu*

(*The History of the Former Han*) reveals that 'because he slew so many officers and soldiers the Sui river ceased to flow'. A change of tactics was clearly necessary against Hsiang Yu's accomplished generalship, and Liu Pang fell back on his natural fortress of Ch'in, the Land within the Passes, from there sending out spies to ferment trouble on Hsiang Yu's territories and soldiers to relieve other kings under pressure. The strategic advantage of the Wei river valley told again. Whereas Hsiang Yu was obliged to dash from one place to another in order to maintain his authority, and at the same time constantly suffer from shortages of supplies, Liu Pang drew on the agricultural resources of his stronghold, and quietly awaited his opponent's collapse. This came in 202 BC. Never defeated on the battlefield, Hsiang Yu discovered to his horror that he had frittered away his strength. His belligerent arrogance had cost him all his support. He died fleeing with a detachment of cavalry from his camp near P'eng Ch'eng.

The humble Liu Pang had beaten the aristocratic Hsiang Yu. The *Ch'ien-Han Shu* recalls the unusual physiognomy of Liu Pang, his prominent nose, 'dragon forehead' and the 'seventy-two black moles' on his left thigh, as well as the scaly dragon that appeared to his mother at his conception, but it cannot disguise the historical fact of a peasant background. The first Han emperor, Kao-tsu or 'High Ancestor' as his reigning title means, was probably illiterate and not a little intolerant of scholars. His accession can be looked upon as a popular movement. China must have breathed a sigh of relief that the years of repression and violence were over. A commoner had fought his way to the imperial throne for the first time in Chinese history. The measures which Ch'in Shih-huang-ti had adopted to weaken feudalism proved so thorough and effective that in the moment of Ch'in's humiliation all attempts to re-establish the old order failed. The civil war between the rebel leaders left a peasant as the Son of Heaven.

Although Emperor Han Kao-tsu realized that Ch'in policy was correct in reducing everything 'in a uniform manner', the need for tact and diplomacy was not lost on him. On the throne he neither aped aristocratic manners nor slackened his compassion for the ordinary people, and though his earthy vocabulary unsettled polite courtiers, he had the wit to appreciate the value of learned and cultivated assistants and advisers. His strongest supporters were the *shih* and the *nung*; the scholars who provided the manpower for the imperial civil service and the peasant farmers who supplied tax-grain and labour. In reaction against Legalist practice, Emperor Han Kao-tsu acknowledged that in decision-making a ruler must heed his officials and that government exists for the benefit of the people. From the outset the Han empire was a compromise that reflected the uncertain political conditions after the fall of the Ch'in dynasty. Emperor Han Kao-tsu left to his successors the elimination of the quasi-feudalism he had inherited. While he allowed surviving aristocratic families to own lands, and even granted fiefs to his own supporters and relations, these holdings were small and contained within the imperial framework of provinces, which were controlled by governors and magistrates after the Ch'in pattern.

The administrative system which the Han emperors took over from the Ch'in proved to be one of the most stable frameworks for social order ever developed. Despite the initial association with totalitarianism, the Chinese succeeded in evolving from it a bureaucratic government staffed by educated men. The model official after 202 BC was to be the Confucian scholar. He was a man firm in principle and benevolent in outlook; he served the throne and protected the ordinary people. It is not a little ironic that the single-minded autocracy of Ch'in Shih-huang-ti gave place to the Celestial Empire so admired by the European Enlightenment. 'A remarkable fact and quite worthy as marking a difference from the West', Matteo Ricci wrote seventeen hundred years later, 'is that the entire kingdom is administered by the Order of the Learned, the Philosophers. The responsibility for orderly management of the entire realm is wholly and completely committed to their charge and care.' How vexed Li Ssu would have been to learn that the labours of a lifetime had inadvertently established a unified and enlightened empire in which the creative genius of Chinese civilization could flower. In his death cell he foresaw the collapse of the Ch'in dynasty: 'Outlaws will come to Hsienyang, and deer wander through the palace courtyard.' But he had no inkling of the second empire to be founded by the socially insignificant Liu Pang. Nor would he have expected to see a new imperial capital arise in 200 BC at Ch'ang-an, across the Wei river from Hsienyang. The last word on Ch'in belongs perhaps to the Han scholar and statesman Chia I, who offered, fifty years after the event, this telling reason for its overthrow by the first peasant rebellion in Chinese history. Chia I said Ch'in fell because it failed 'to realize that the power to conquer and the power to hold what has been won are not the same'.

CHRONOLOGIES

General

c. 1765–1027 BC	SHANG DYNASTY
1027–256 BC	CHOU DYNASTY
1027–771 BC	Western Chou period
770–481 BC	Ch'un Ch'iu period
481–221 BC	Chan Kuo period
221–207/206 BC	CH'IN DYNASTY
206/202 BC–AD 220	HAN DYNASTY
206/202 BC–AD 9	Former Han period
AD 24–220	Later Han Period

Ch'in (300–200 BC)

c. 300 BC	A long wall is built by Ch'in to resist the north-western nomads.
285 BC	Threatened rebellion in Shu leads to the incorporation of the territory in the state of Ch'in.
c. 280 BC	Birth in Ch'u of Li Ssu, the future Grand Councillor of the First Emperor of China.
c. 261 BC	The merchant Lu Pu-wei befriends in Han-tan the hostage Ch'in prince Tzu-chu, the father of the First Emperor.
260 BC	Battle of Ch'ang P'ing. Ch'in slaughters 400,000 Chao prisoners on the battlefield.
c. 258 BC	Birth of Cheng, the future First Emperor.
257 BC	Ch'in throws a great bridge across the Yellow river.
256 BC	The Chou king, the Son of Heaven, deposed by Ch'in troops.
251 BC	King Hsiao-wen summons Prince Tzu-chu and Lu Pu-wei to Hsienyang.
250 BC	Prince Tzu-chu succeeds to the throne of Ch'in as King Chuang-hsiang. Lu Pu-wei is appointed as his Grand Councillor.
250–240 BC	Li Ping inaugurates the great Min river conservancy scheme in Shu.
248 BC	Birth of Liu Pang, the future first Han emperor Kao-tsu.
247 BC	Death of King Chuang-hsiang. Li Ssu leaves Hsun-tzu for Ch'in.
246 BC	The thirteen-year-old Cheng ascends the Ch'in throne. 'Uncle' Lu Pu-wei acts as regent. Li Ssu is made a senior scribe by King Cheng. The Chengkuo canal is opened.

238 BC	Rebellion of Lao Ai and debasement of Lu Pu-wei.
237 BC	Lu Pu-wei is exiled to Shu, where he commits suicide two years later.
	Li Ssu saved from deportation along with other aliens through his memorial to the throne.
237–219 BC	Li Ssu acts as justice minister.
233 BC	Han Fei-tzu dies in Hsienyang.
230 BC	Ch'in annexes Han.
228 BC	Ch'in annexes Chao.
227 BC	Unsuccessful attempt by Ching K'o to assassinate King Cheng.
225 BC	Ch'in annexes Wei.
223 BC	General Wang Chien finally subdues Ch'u, which Ch'in annexes.
222 BC	Ch'in annexes Yen.
221 BC	Ch'in annexes Ch'i, the last feudal state in the Middle Kingdom.
	To mark the unification of China King Cheng assumes the title Ch'in Shih-huang-ti, the First Emperor.
	Li Ssu recommends the abolition of feudalism.
	The First Emperor promulgates a uniform code of law, standardizes currency, weights and measures, as well as the written language, and establishes a centralized state governed through a non-hereditary bureaucracy.
	The empire is divided into thirty-six, later forty-two, commanderies garrisoned by Ch'in troops and connected by a network of roads.
	Weapons are collected and melted down at Hsienyang.
	The influence of Taoist magic on the First Emperor becomes apparent.
	The Mount Li tomb is first mentioned.
219 BC	The First Emperor tours the empire.
	He also tries to obtain the elixir of immortality.
	Li Ssu becomes Grand Councillor and head of the imperial administration.
	Kao Chien-Li fails to assassinate the First Emperor.
218 BC	Unsuccessful attempt by Chang Liang to assassinate the First Emperor during a tour of inspection.
215 BC	Second search for the elixir of immortality commissioned by the First Emperor.
	Victory of General Meng T'ien over the northern nomads.
214 BC	Meng T'ien is mentioned as building the Great Wall. Like the imperial road system, this gigantic task was not, of course, the work of a single year.
213 BC	Speech of Shun-yu Yueh causes Li Ssu to demand the Burning of the Books.
212 BC	The First Emperor kills 460 scholars at Hsienyang and banishes his eldest son, Prince Fu-su, to the Great Wall. The A-fang palace is started.
210 BC	Nan-hai is annexed and pacified.
	The First Emperor dies on a tour of inspection.
	Chao Kao and Li Ssu force Fu-su and Meng T'ien to die, bring back the body of the deceased ruler to the capital as if he were alive, and there announce the funeral and the accession of Hu-hai, a worthless younger son.
209 BC	The Second Emperor, Erh Shih-huang-ti, purges the imperial family, the court and the imperial bureaucracy. Chao Kao secretly influences the young emperor.
	Rebellion of Ch'en She and Wu Kang, the first peasant leaders in Chinese history.
208 BC	Chang Han successfully deals with the rebellion but is soon engulfed by further risings. In the battle of Ting-t'ao the southern rebel leader Hsiang Liang falls.

Chao Kao becomes dominant at Hsienyang.

Li Ssu is executed.

207 BC   Chang Han joins the rebels.

The Hsin-an massacre accounts for 200,000 Ch'in soldiers.

Chao Kao presents a stag to the Second Emperor and two weeks afterwards compels the ruler to commit suicide.

Accession of Tzu-ying, nephew of the Second Emperor, and death of Chao Kao.

Battle of Lan-t'ien gives Liu Pang control of the Wei river valley.

206 BC   King Tzu-ying submits to Liu Pang.

The rebel forces under Hsiang Yu destroy Hsienyang and desecrate the tomb of the First Emperor.

After the division of the empire between the rebel leaders, Liu Pang seizes the Land within the Passes.

205 BC   Hsiang Yu defeats Liu Pang near P'eng Ch'eng.

202 BC   Death of Hsiang Yu.

The Han empire comes into being with Liu Pang enthroned as Emperor Kao-tsu.

'A general amnesty for the world' is proclaimed.

200 BC   Ch'ang-an, across the Wei river from the ruins of Hsienyang, is made the Han capital.

BIBLIOGRAPHY

It remains a misfortune of Chinese Studies in the English-speaking world that 'we still lack an edition of the *Shih Chi* of Ssu-ma Ch'ien. There are several translations of parts of the monumental work of the Han historian, but nothing to compare with Homer Dubs's splendid critical edition of Pan Ku's *Ch'ien-Han Shu* (*The History of the Former Han Dynasty*). Here Dubs provides the Chinese text, a parallel translation, and detailed notes. For this reason the interested reader will find it necessary to consult several books if he wishes to go beyond the present translations. Given below are two lists of references, the first in Chinese, the second in European languages. The colossal ceramic figures uncovered at Mount Li have revealed the paucity of books on the Ch'in dynasty published in the West.

In Chinese

SSU-MA CH'IEN
  Shih Chi, Chung Hua Publishing Company edition, Shanghai, 1923; reissued during the 1960s in Hongkong.
  It includes the original text of the *Historical Records* as well as later commentaries.

THE MOUNT LI FINDS
  These are admirably recorded in two journals, *Wenwu* (*Cultural Relics*) and *Kaogu* (*Archaeology*), both of which are published in Peking.
  The relevant issues are as follows:
  Kaogu, 1962/8; *Wenwu*, 1964/9; *Wenwu*, 1973/5; *Wenwu*, 1975/1; *Kaogu*, 1975/6; *Wenwu*, 1975/11; *Wenwu*, 1978/5; *Wenwu*, 1979/12

In European Languages

BARNARD, N. *The nature of the Ch'in 'Reform of the Script' as reflected in archaeological documents excavated under conditions of control,* in Roy, D. T. and Tsien, Tsuen-hsuin (eds.), *Ancient China: Studies in Early Civilization*, Hongkong, 1978.

BODDE, D. *China's First Unifier. A study of the Ch'in dynasty as seen in the life of Li Ssu (c. 280–208 BC)*, Leiden, 1938; Sinica Leidensia 3; reprinted in Hongkong, 1967; *Statesman, Patriot, and General in Ancient China.*

Three 'Shih Chi' biographies of the Ch'in dynasty (255–206 BC),
New Haven, 1940; American Oriental Society 17; reprinted New York, 1967.
This volume contains translations and discussion of the lives of
Lu Pu-wei, Ching K'o, and Meng T'ien.

BYNNER, W. *The Way of Life according to Lao Tzu*, New York, 1962.

CHANG, Kwang-chih. *The Archaeology of Ancient China*,
3rd revised edition, New Haven, 1977.

CHAVANNES, E. *Les Mémoires historiques de Se-ma Ts'ien*,
5 volumes, Paris, 1895 till 1905.

CHI, Ch'ao-ting. *Key Economic Areas in Chinese History,*
as revealed in the Development of Public Works for Water-Control,
London, 1936; reprinted, New York, 1970.

COTTERELL, Y. Y. and A. B. *The Early Civilization of China*,
London and New York, 1975.

CREEL, H. G. *Confucius and the Chinese Way*, New York, 1960;
originally published as *Confucius; the Man and the Myth*, New York, 1949;
London, 1951.

CRUMP, J. I. Jr. *Chan-kuo Ts'e*, Oxford, 1970.

DUBS, H. H. (with the assistance of Jen T'ai and P'an Lo-chi)
The History of the Former Han Dynasty by Pan ku,
a critical translation with annotations,
3 volumes, Baltimore, 1938, 1944 and 1955.
Excellent for the collapse of the Ch'in dynasty and the rise of
Liu Pang, the first Han emperor.
Hsun Tzu; the Moulder of Ancient Confucianism, London, 1927;
Probsthain's Oriental Series 15.

DUYVENDAK, J. J. L. *The Book of Lord Shang. A Classic of the School of Law*,
London, 1928; reprinted 1963.

GRANET, M. *La Religion des Chinois*, Paris, 1922.

GRIFFITH, S. B. *Sun Tzu. The Art of War*, Oxford, 1963.

HSU, Cho-yun. *Ancient China in Transition. An Analysis of Social Mobility,*
722–222 BC, Stanford, 1965.

HSIAO, Kung-chuan. *A History of Chinese Political Thought.*
Volume 1; From the Beginnings to the Sixth Century AD,
trans. F. W. Mote, Princeton, 1979.
This work is a mine of information on the Ch'un Ch'iu and Chan Kuo periods,
and especially good on Kuan Chung, Shen Pu-hai, Chuang-tzu, Shang Yang
and Han Fei-tzu.

KIERMAN, F. A. Jr. and FAIRBANK, J. K. *Chinese Ways in Warfare*,
Harvard, 1974.

LAU, D. C. *Mencius*, Harmondsworth, 1970.

LEGGE, J. *Shu Ching, Book of History, a modernized edition of the translations of James Legge by Clae Waltham*, London 1972.

LI, Yu-ning. *The First Emperor of China. The Politics of Historiography*, White Plains, N.Y., 1975.

LIAO, W. K. *The Complete Works of Han Fei Tzu. A Classic of Chinese Political Science*, 2 volumes, London, 1939; reprinted 1959; Probsthain's Oriental Series 25 and 26.

MACGOWAN, H. *The Imperial History of China*, London, 1897; reprinted 1973.

MASPERO, H. *La Chine Antique*, Paris, 1927; reprinted 1955.

MEI, Yi-pao. *Motse. The Neglected Rival of Confucius*, London, 1934; Probsthain's Oriental Series 20.

MEI, Yi-pao. *The Ethical and Political Works of Motse*, London, 1929; Probsthain's Oriental Series 19.

NEEDHAM, J. *Science and Civilization in China, 2: The History of Scientific Thought*, Cambridge, 1956. This amazing survey of ancient Chinese ideas explains the School of Nature (*yin-yang chia*).

RUBIN, V. A. *Individual and State in Ancient China. Essays on Four Chinese Philosophers; Confucius, Mo Tzu, Shang Yang and Chuang Tzu*, trans. S. I. Levine, New York, 1976. This is an English version of Rubin's *Ideologiia i kul'tura drevnego kitaia (Ideology and Culture in Ancient China)*, Moscow, 1970.

SMITH, D. H. *Confucius*, London, 1973.

SWANN, N. L. *Food and Money in Ancient China. The Earliest Economic History of China to AD 25. Han Shu 24, with related texts, Han Shu 91 and Shih Chi 129*, Princeton, 1950.

TREGEAR, T. R. *A Geography of China*, London, 1965.

TSCHEPPE, A. *Histoire du Royaume de Ts'in*, Shanghai, 1909; Variétés sinologiques 27.

WALEY, A. *The Way and its Power. A Study of the Tao Teh Ching and its Place in Chinese Thought*, London, 1934.

WANG, Yu-ch'uan. *Early Chinese Coinage*, New York, 1951; American Numismatic Society 16.

WATSON, B. *Records of the Grand Historian of China* (from the *Shih Chi* of Ssu-ma Ch'ien), 2 volumes, New York, 1961. It covers the fall of the Ch'in dynasty and the rise of Han dynasty. *Ssu-ma Ch'ien, Grand Historian of China*, New York, 1958;

Records of the Historian. Chapters from the 'Shih Chi' of Ssu-ma Ch'ien,
New York, 1965.
This contains the biographies of Lu Pu-wei, Ching K'o, Hsiang Yu and the
Han emperor Kao-tsu.

WATSON, W. *China. Before the Han Dynasty*, London, 1961;
The Genius of China, London, 1973.
The catalogue of the Chinese Exhibition.

YANG, Hsien-yi and Gladys. *Records of the Historian,
written by Szuma Chien*, Hongkong, 1974.
This contains the biographies of Confucius, Shang Yang, Lu Pu-wei,
the First Emperor, Ch'en She, and Hsiang Yu.

LIST OF MAPS AND PLANS

Page 19   The tomb of the First Emperor at Mount Li

20–1   Plan of Pit No. 1

22   Cross-sectional view of three corridors of Pit No. 1

38   Sketchmap of a corridor of Pit No. 2

38   Plan of Pit No. 2

40   Plan of Pit No. 3

41   Sketch layout of warriors in Pit No. 3

57   Drawing of the A-fang palace

61   Sketchmap of Sian area

66–7   Drawing of a Ch'in palace in Hsienyang

92   The major states of the Ch'un Ch'iu period (770–481 BC)

102   Chan Kuo China (481–221 BC)

115   Plan of Han-tan

138   The Ch'in Empire

ACKNOWLEDGMENTS

Colour illustration acknowledgments

The page numbers given are those opposite the colour plates, or,
in the case of a double-page spread, those either side of the plate.

Pages 24, 25, 89, 120 and 121; jacket front and back: The Museum of Pottery Figures of
Warriors and Horses
from the Tomb of Ch'in Shih-huang-ti

24–5, 88 overleaf above, and 168–9: New China News Agency

88, 88 overleaf below, 89 previous page above and below, and 168:
Frank Spooner Pictures (Photo: Gamma/Lothon)

120–1 and 169: The Rainbird Publishing Group Limited

Acknowledgments, continued

Black and white illustration acknowledgments

The author and the producers of the book would like to thank the following
Chinese authorities for permission to reproduce the photographs on pages
23, 24, 25 (above right), 26, 27, 37, 42–3, 46, 48, 50–1, 66, 68 (above),
70, 79, 150, 151 (above), and 189

The Museum of Pottery Figures of Warriors and Horses
from the Tomb of Ch'in Shih-huang-ti
The Shensi Provincial Museum
The Hsienyang Municipal Museum

Also
Robert Harding Associates: Pages: 36, 74–5 and 76
The School of Oriental and African Studies Library: Frontispiece
Frank Spooner Pictures (Photo: Gamma/Lothon): Pages 49 (above) and 151
(below)
The Rainbird Publishing Group Limited: Pages 11, 16, 19 (above), 28, 30, 31,
33, 34–5, 49 (below), 54–5, 56–7, 59, 62–3, 68 (below), 71 (below), 72–3, 74
(below), 137, 144, 148, 149, 154, 159 and 170; back jacket flap

Artwork credits

Brian and Constance Dear: Pages 20–1, 22, 38, 40, 41 and 66–7
Eugene Fleury: Pages 19 (below), 57, 61, 92, 102 and 138
Michael Kelly: Pages 25 (above left), 29, 32, 39, 44, 47, 52, 67 and 71 (above)
Maire Smith: Pages 120–1

PERMISSIONS

The author and producers of the book would like to thank the following publishers for permission to quote extracts of their work. The page numbers refer to those in *The First Emperor of China*.

Page 85   George Allen and Unwin Ltd, London from
        Shu Ching: Book of History. A modernized edition of the translations of James Legge
        by Clae Waltham.

Pages 86 and 174 E. J. Brill, Leiden from
        China's First Unifier: A Study of the Ch'in dynasty as seen in the Life of Li Ssu
        by Derk Bodde.

Page 171   Cambridge University Press from
        Science and Civilisation in China, Vol. 4, Part 3, Civil Engineering and Nautics
        by Joseph Needham.

Pages 125, 127, 132 and 141 Columbia University Press, New York from
        Basic Writings of Mo Tzu, Hsun Tzu and Han Fei Tzu,
        translated by Burton Watson.

Page 87   Grove Press Inc, New York from
        Anthology of Chinese Literature,
        edited by C. Birch.

Page 44   Oxford University Press from
        Sun Tzu, The Art of War,
        translated by S. B. Griffith.

Page 69   Oxford University Press from
        Chan-Kuo Ts'e,
        translated by J. I. Crump, Jnr.

Pages 90 and 126 Princeton University Press, New Jersey from
        A History of Chinese Political Thought, Vol. 1, From the Beginnings to the Sixth Century AD
        by Kung-Chuan Hsiao, translated by F. W. Mote.

Page 105 Arthur Probsthain and Co, London from
        The Book of Lord Shang
        by J. J. L. Duyvendak.

INDEX

A-fang palace, 12, 57, 58, 59, 60, 74, 77, 175, 181
agriculture, 12, 57–8, 60, 69, 87, 88, 90, 97, 106, 118, 152, 172; changes during Chan Kuo period, 69, 90, 118; water-conservancy schemes, 58, 77–8, 109, 110, 111
ancestor worship, 84, 86, 94, 95, 114, 121, 127, 128, 139, 181
An-kuo (crown prince of Ch'in) *see* Hsiao-wen
Anyang (last capital of Shang dynasty), 84
archaeological discoveries *see* Hsienyang *and* Mount Li
aristocracy, 12, 46, 64, 65, 85, 86, 87, 96, 99, 101, 103, 122, 127, 167, 168, 173, 188; abolition of hereditary system in Ch'in, 46, 105, 107, 108, 109, 112; concentration in Hsienyang, 12, 64, 65; downgrading during Chan Kuo period, 103 *see also* feudalism

barbarians, 84, 95, 97, 98, 103, 147, 149, 154, 158, 160, 164, 172; and Ch'in, 97, 98, 147, 149, 154, 158; from the northern steppes (the Hsiung Nu or Huns), 98, 103, 147, 149, 154, 155, 158
battles: Ch'ang Ping (259 BC), 117, 183; Ch'eng-p'u (632 BC), 93, 94, 95; Hsin-an (207 BC), 183; Lan-t'ien (207 BC), 188; P'eng Ch'eng (205 BC), 190; Pi (595 BC), 95, 96; T'ing-tao (208 BC), 182; Yen-ling (575 BC), 95
Book of Documents (*Shu Ching*), 84, 85, 119, 123
Book of Lord Shang (*Shang-chun shu*), 105, 106
Book of Poetry (*Shih Ching*), 87, 122
Book of Rights (*Li Chi*), 86
bridges, 111, 112
bronze, 27, 67, 89, 90

Burning of the Books (213 BC) 6, 12, 120, 133, 153, 163–4, 168, 187

canals, 10, 58, 88, 89, 110, 141; Chengkuo canal, 78, 110, 111, 141; importance of, in Chinese history, 58; Magic canal, 156; Min river system, 110
cavalry, 10, 38, 39, 103; in Pit No. 2 at Mount Li, 38, 39 *see also* military tactics
Chan Kuo period (481–221 BC), 27, 44, 45, 46, 69, 90, 97, 100, 101–17, 119, 120, 123, 130, 150, 168, 171
Chan-kuo T'se (*Intrigues of the Warring States*), 69, 101, 114
Ch'ang-an (imperial capital from 200 BC), 192
Chang Han (Ch'in general), 43, 180, 182, 183
Chang-hsiang (king of Ch'in, 306–251 BC), 69
Chang Liang (would-be assassin of the First Emperor), 145
Chao (feudal state), 9, 93, 101, 103, 104, 107, 112, 115, 117, 142, 143, 145, 150, 158, 164, 183
Chao Kao (eunuch), 154, 156, 165, 166, 174, 175, 177, 178, 179, 181, 182, 183, 184, 185, 186, 187, 188
Chao Liang (hermit), 118, 119
chariots *see* weapons and armour *as well as* military tactics
Chen She (first leader of a peasant rebellion), 12, 166, 180, 181, 182
Cheng (king of Ch'in) *see* the First Emperor
Chengkuo canal *see* canals
Cheng Kuo (hydraulic engineer), 9, 110, 111, 142, 163
Ch'i (feudal state), 88, 89, 93, 95, 98, 100, 101, 110, 115, 117, 119, 123, 131, 136, 140, 164, 171, 190; and the hegemon system, 88, 91, 92
Chia I (Han statesman), 107, 108, 109, 192–3
Ch'ien-Han Shu (*History of the Former Han Dynasty*), 152, 190–1
Chin (feudal state), 92, 93, 94, 95, 96, 100, 101, 122; collapse of (403 BC), 93, 98, 101; rivalry with Ch'in and Ch'u, 94, 95, 96, 97, 98, 100, 101
Ch'in (feudal state, dynasty, and empire), 9, 10, 17, 25, 40, 42, 44, 45, 57, 58, 61, 74, 75, 90, 93, 95, 97, 98, 99, 100, 101, 104, 105, 107, 109, 110, 112, 113, 114, 116, 117, 118, 119,

122, 124, 125, 131, 132, 136, 139, 140, 141, 142, 143, 144, 145, 147, 150, 152, 153, 156, 157, 158, 160, 161, 162, 163, 164, 165, 166, 167, 168, 173, 174, 178, 181, 182, 183, 185, 186, 187, 188, 191, 192, 193; and Legalism, 104, 105, 106, 111, 119, 131, 132, 133; authoritarianism of, 105, 112, 119, 125, 132, 133, 161, 164, 167–8, 174, 181, 183, 192; favourable geographical position of, 69, 77, 78, 98; *hsien* in, 109, 150, 167; military organization of, 10, 22, 24, 25, 40, 42, 44, 45, 46, 52; 103, 117, 146–7, 183; origins of, 97; reformed by Shang Yang, 9, 105, 106, 107, 108, 109; relative backwardness of, 9, 97, 119
Ch'in Shih huang-ti *see* the First Emperor
Ch'in Wu-yang (accomplice of Ching K'o), 143
Ching K'o (would-be assassin of the First Emperor), 142, 143, 144, 145, 162
Chiu-yuan (city), 154
Chou (feudal state and dynasty), 77, 84, 85, 86, 88, 89, 92, 93, 94, 97, 100, 101, 117, 128, 139, 164, 168, 169; abandonment of first capital (771 BC), 85, 97, 169; fall of dynasty (256 BC), 117
Ch'u (feudal state), 44, 46, 88, 93, 95, 96, 97, 98, 99, 100, 101, 103, 109, 117, 127, 129, 145, 146, 147, 150, 166, 171, 182, 188, 190; rivalry with Ch'in for supremacy, 44, 97, 98, 101, 109, 117, 145, 146, 147; struggle against nearby Wu, 99, 100, 145
Chu-lu (city), 182
Chuang (duke of Ch'u), 98, 100
Chuang-hsiang (king of Ch'in and father of the First Emperor), 9, 113, 114, 115, 116
Chuang-tzu (Taoist philosopher), 129
Ch'un Ch'iu period (770–481 BC), 84–100, 103, 115, 116, 120
coinage, 10, 116, 150, 152, 172, 173; Ch'in unification of, 10, 116, 150, 172, 173
commerce, 87, 89, 115, 116, 118, 150, 152, 172, 173; measures against trade, 172, 173 *see also shang*
Confucius and Confucianism (*ju chia*), 87, 96–7, 99, 107, 108, 118, 120, 121, 122, 124, 126, 128, 131, 153, 154,

161, 163, 164, 165, 169, 171, 174, 192; ancestor worship in, 121; and education, 121, 124; and feudalism, 87, 120, 121, 153, 163–4, 165; and human sacrifice, 127; and the family, 99, 108, 123, 128, 165; and the supernatural, 121, 124, 161; *chun-tzu* (superior man), 122
crossbows *see* weapons and armour

Erh Shih huang-ti *see* the Second Emperor
expulsion of aliens from Ch'in (237 BC), 163

fa (Legalist concept of positive law), 106, 131, 132
feudalism, 12, 46, 64, 84, 85, 86, 87, 92, 93, 95, 96, 97, 99, 101, 103, 104, 105, 107, 109, 112, 120, 121, 122, 124, 125, 126, 127, 149, 163–4, 165, 167, 168, 173, 188, 191; abolition of, by Li Ssu, 64–5, 86, 149, 153, 163–4, 165, 167, 168, 173, 188, 191; decay of, 85, 92, 93, 95, 100, 101, 102, 104, 105, 107, 109, 112, 123, 124; highest point of, 84
First Emperor (Ch'in Shih-huang-ti), 6, 9, 10, 12, 17, 18, 40, 45, 53, 58, 60, 70, 75, 77, 78, 90, 98, 107, 109, 113, 114, 115, 117, 120, 124, 130, 131, 132, 133, 136–57, 158, 160, 163, 164, 171, 172, 173, 177, 178, 179, 181, 188, 191, 192; attempted assassinations of, 12, 142–5, 156, 162; attitude towards scholars, 12, 109, 115, 120, 153–4; birth of, 9, 113; character of, 10, 45, 58, 65, 75, 77, 117, 131, 140, 145, 153, 156, 160, 161; comes to the throne as King Cheng, 113, 140; death and funerary arrangements of, 12, 17, 18, 28, 37, 53, 58, 60, 145, 156, 157, 178, 188; inscriptions of, 12, 78–81, 172; policies of, 9, 10, 64–5, 75, 86, 132, 149, 150, 153, 154, 155, 158, 160, 163, 164, 167, 168, 171, 172, 173, 191; quest for immortality by, 12, 130, 131, 140, 145, 153; relations with Li Ssu, 65, 86, 141, 149, 153, 156, 160, 161, 162, 163, 167, 168, 173, 179; title of, 9, 136–9, 140, 147, 157
Five Elements (*wu hsing*), 75, 77, 131, *see also* Taoism
Fu-su (Ch'in prince), 154, 157, 165, 167, 177

Gobi desert, 147
Great Wall, 6, 11, 37, 58, 60, 111, 147, 154, 155, 156, 158, 168, 171

Han (dynasty and empire), 61, 90, 96–7, 119, 120, 122, 124, 127, 150, 165, 167, 169, 171, 172, 173, 174, 182, 187, 188, 191, 192
Han (feudal state), 93, 101, 103, 104, 107, 110, 111, 117, 119, 132, 141, 145, 164
Han Fei-tzu (Legalist philosopher), 91, 104, 119, 124, 132, 133, 141, 142, 166, 168; admired by the First Emperor, 104, 141, 142; his death in a Hsienyang prison, 104, 142
Han T'an (eunuch), 187
Han-tan (city), 9, 112, 116, 145
Han Wu-ti (Emperor, 141–87 BC), 167
Hao (city), 85, 97, 169
hegemon system (*pa*), 88, 91, 92, 93, 97, 98, 100, 119
Hsia (semi-legendary dynasty), 126, 128, 129–30
Hsia-tu (city), 116
Hsia Wu-chu (the First Emperor's physician), 144, 145
Hsiang Liang (rebel leader), 182, 188
Hsiang Yu (chief rebel leader), 17, 182, 183, 187, 188, 190, 191
Hsiao (king of Ch'in, 361–338 BC), 9, 105
Hsiao-wen (king of Ch'in, *c.* 251 BC), 112
hsien (prefectures) *see* Ch'in
Hsienmen Kao (Taoist adept), 130
Hsienyang (Ch'in capital), 12, 56–78, 108, 109, 113, 115, 116, 120, 143, 145, 150, 152, 154, 156, 157, 158, 161, 162, 168, 171, 175, 178, 179, 180, 181, 182, 183, 184, 186, 187, 188, 190, 192
Hsu Fu (leader of a sea-borne expedition to the immortals), 130, 156
Hsun-tzu (heterodox Confucian philosopher), 122, 123, 124, 130, 140, 161, 162, 166; and 'human portents', 161, 166; on rites, 124, 125; view of human nature, 124; visit to Ch'in, 124–5
Huai river, 96
Huan (duke of Ch'i and first hegemon), 88, 89, 91, 92, 93, 101, 110, 119
Huang-ti (legendary Yellow

Emperor), 139–40, 162
Hu-hai *see* the Second Emperor

immortals and immortality, 12, 130, 131, 140; drug of deathlessness (*pu su chih ts'ao*), 12, 130, 131, 140; the First Emperor's quest for immortality, 12, 130, 131, 140; *hsien* (immortals), 12, 130, 140
iron, 27, 67, 89, 90, 145, 152

Kao Chien-li (would-be assassin of the First Emperor), 145
Kuan Chung (statesman), 89, 90, 91, 92, 131; his *Kuan Tzu*, 90, 91, 93, 131
kung (artisans), 87

Land within the Passes (the Wei river valley), 58, 77, 98, 191; as the impregnable Ch'in heartland, 69, 78, 98, 191; its loess soil, 77, 78
Lao Ai (rebellion of), 113, 114, 163
Lao-tzu (Taoist philosopher), 128, 129
Legalism (*fa chia*), 91, 99, 104, 106, 107, 111, 114, 115, 119, 120, 122, 124, 125, 129, 131, 132, 141, 152, 156, 164, 165, 166, 167, 168, 173, 174, 192; authoritarianism of, 91, 105, 106, 108, 132, 133, 141, 166, 167, 168; belief in harsh punishments, 104, 105, 106, 108, 132, 141, 166; dislike of artistic pursuits, 106–7, 133, 164; emphasis on agriculture and war, 106, 107, 111, 141, 152
li (Confucian concept of rites), 121, 125
Lieh-tzu (Taoist philosopher), 139
Li Ping (Ch'in governor of Shu-Pa), 109, 110
Li Ssu (statesman), 9, 65, 86, 104, 107, 115, 124, 131, 133, 136, 140, 141, 142, 152, 153, 154, 156, 157, 158–76, 177, 179, 181, 182, 183, 185, 186, 188, 192; and the abolition of feudalism, 65, 86, 149, 163, 164, 165, 188; arrives in Hsienyang, 113, 160, 162; Burning of the Books, 6, 133, 153–4, 163–4, 168; fall and death of, 167, 174, 175, 179, 182; influence with the First Emperor 65, 86, 153, 156, 160, 161, 162, 163, 164, 167, 168, 179; plots with Chao Kao, 154, 157, 165–6, 167; rivalry with Han Fei-tzu, 104, 142; unification of the

script, 160, 164, 168–71
Li Yu (eldest son of Li Ssu), 179
Lin-tzu (city), 93, 116, 136
Liu Pang (first Han emperor of Kao-tzu), 165, 172, 178, 180–1, 182, 183, 187, 188, 189, 190, 191, 192; clemency of, 188; invasion of Ch'in, 178, 182, 187, 188; peasant background, 189, 191, 192; struggle with Hsiang Yu, 188, 189, 190, 191
Loyang (city), 85, 88, 94, 97, 98, 100, 101, 128, 169
Lu (feudal state), 88, 93, 100, 121, 126
Lu (scholar-magician from Yen), 130, 156, 158, 160
Lu Pu-wei (merchant and statesman), 109, 112, 113, 114, 115, 116, 119, 120, 140, 141, 162, 163, 173; befriends the First Emperor's father, 112, 140; fall and death of, 113, 114, 140–1; his Lu-shih Ch'un-ch'iu, 115, 120; regent for King Cheng, 113, 140–1

Mencius (Confucian philosopher), 88, 122, 123, 124, 125, 127; and human goodness, 122–3, 124; deplores feudal aggression, 123; doctrine of justified rebellion, 123
Meng Chiang-nu (legend of), 155
Meng T'ien (Ch'in general), 154, 157, 158, 165, 166, 171
military tactics: Ch'un Ch'iu period, 45, 46, 93–6, 100; Chan Kuo period, 27, 44, 45, 46, 100, 101, 103, 105, 117, 126–7, 145–6; of Ch'in armies, 10, 22, 24, 25, 40, 42, 44, 45, 52, 65–6, 69, 98, 117, 146–7, 180, 182, 183
Mo-tzu and Moism (mo chia), 120, 125, 126, 127, 128, 129
Mount Li (site of the First Emperor's tomb), 6, 12, 13, 16–53, 55, 58, 65, 74, 90, 157, 178, 179, 180; discovery of terracotta army, 6, 20, 37; funerary palace, 18; kneeling figures found near tomb, 37; mausoleum site, 16, 17, 18, 20, 37, 53; pottery pits, 10, 13, 20–48: No. 1, 20, 21, 22, 24, 25, 28, 37, 40–5; No. 2, 27, 37, 38, 39, 45, 48; No. 3, 37, 39; No. 4, 37; prospects for new discoveries, 37, 53

Naturalists (yin-yang chia), 131
nung (peasant farmers), 87, 88, 90, 149, 154, 173, 192

Ordos desert, 154, 158

P'ing (king of Chou), 85, 86, 89

rebellions against Ch'in dynasty, 12, 17, 21, 42–3, 59, 60, 65, 166, 174, 177, 180, 182, 183, 184, 188, 189, 193
roads, 152–3, 171–2

San Ch'uan (city), 179
Second Emperor (Erh Shih-huang-ti), 12, 17, 18, 42, 60, 152, 157, 160, 165, 166, 173–4, 175, 177, 178, 179, 180, 181, 184, 185, 186, 187; death of, 12, 185, 186, 187; indifference to affairs of state, 166, 173, 174, 177, 181, 184
Shang (dynasty), 84, 97, 121, 136, 164, 169
shang (merchants), 87, 112, 113, 119, 120, 172, 173, 174
Shang-ch'iu (city), 93, 94, 100
Shang-lin park, 74, 184
Shang Yang (philosopher and statesman), 9, 91, 104, 105, 106, 107, 108, 109, 111, 118, 132, 166, 175; ascendancy in Ch'in, 9, 105; fall and death of, 105–6, 175; policies of, 9, 105, 106, 107, 108, 109
Shantung (province), 77
Shen Pu-hai (statesman), 104, 132, 166, 168
Shensi (province), 16, 20, 40, 53, 60, 61
shih (scholar-gentry), 87, 103, 113, 114, 119, 120, 127, 153, 154, 164, 165, 172, 191, 192
Shensi (province), 16, 20, 40, 53, 60, 61
Shih Chi (Historical Records of Ssu-ma Ch'ien), 17, 56, 64, 75, 77, 78, 99, 100, 106, 110, 113, 114, 118, 120, 128, 130, 141, 143, 150, 153–4, 156–7, 158, 160, 163, 166, 168, 179, 183, 184–7, 190
Shu and Pa (modern Szechuan), 58, 78, 109, 110, 113, 188
Shun-yu Yueh (Confucian opponent of Li Ssu), 163, 164, 165, 167
Sian (present-day Ch'ang-an), 8, 16, 57, 59, 77
Sung (feudal state), 92, 93, 95, 100, 103, 126, 150
Sun-tzu (author of The Art of War), 44, 146, 147
Ssu-ma Ch'ien (Han historian), 17, 56, 58, 64, 75, 99, 106, 110, 112, 113, 114, 116, 118, 119, 126, 143, 145, 154, 158, 160, 162, 163, 167, 173, 174, 175, 176, 178, 179, 182, 188

Tan (crown prince of Yen), 142, 143, 145
T'ang (dynasty), 61, 112
Tao Teh Ching (The Way of Virtue), 128
Taoism (tao chia), 16, 115, 120, 126, 128, 129, 139, 140, 153, 158, 161; against feudalism, 128, 129; quest for elixir of life in, 130, 131, 153; rivalry with Confucianism, 128; wu ancestry of, 131
Tso-chuan (Tradition of Tso), 94, 96
Tung Chung-shu (Han scholar), 174
Tzu-chu (father of the First Emperor) see Chuang-hsiang
Tzu-ying (king of Ch'in, 207–206 BC), 12, 178, 185, 187, 188
Tzu-yu (Ch'u general), 94

Wang Chien (veteran Ch'in general), 146, 147
weapons and armour, 10, 22, 25, 39, 48, 66–7, 145, 160; bronze or iron, 27, 67, 89, 90, 145; chariots, 22, 24, 39, 52, 94, 100, 103; crossbows, 22, 48, 103; flexible lances, 22; halberd used by Ch'in infantrymen, 67; iron armour, 27
Wei (feudal state), 93, 97, 101, 103–4, 106, 117, 150, 164
Wei river, 16, 60, 61, 65, 74, 78, 85, 97, 107, 111, 112, 152, 158, 169, 183, 184, 190, 191, 192
Wen (duke of Chin), 92, 93, 94
West river, 155, 156
Wu (feudal state), 93, 99, 100, 145, 171
Wu Ch'en (Ch'u general), 99
Wu Tzu-hsu (Ch'u exile in Wu), 99

Yang Chen Ching (curator of the Museum of Warrior and Horse Figures), 8, 9, 10, 12, 13, 20, 27, 28, 40
Yang-tzu river, 98, 100, 152, 155, 156, 157, 180, 182
Yellow river, 77, 84, 89, 98, 101, 111, 112, 154, 158, 182
Yen (feudal state), 93, 101, 116, 117, 130, 131, 142, 143, 150, 158, 171
Yen Lo (son-in-law of Chao Kao), 184, 185, 186
Yong (city), 64
Yueh (people and feudal state), 93, 99, 100, 145, 155, 160
Yuyang (city), 64